A PRACTICAL INTRODUCTION TO YARN DYEING

D1796411

J. PARK

Chief Executive
Fielding & Johnson Ltd
Abbey Mill   Ross Walk
Leicester LE4 5HH

THE SOCIETY OF DYERS AND COLOURISTS

PERKIN HOUSE   GRATTAN ROAD   BRADFORD   WEST YORKSHIRE

1981

Printed in Great Britain by Allanwood Press Ltd., Stanningley, Pudsey

ISBN 0 901956 28 7

Preface

Despite the increasing volume of technical literature which is produced each year, the comment is often made that there is a lack of papers and textbooks of a practical nature. This mongraph on yarn dyeing practice is an attempt to fill a gap in one area of dyeing technology. The information given is intended to be entirely practical and although much consideration is given to concepts, no apology is made for the omission of theoretical data. This latter information is readily available from the excellent series of books produced by the Society of Dyers and Colourists under the auspices of the Dyers Company Publication Trust.

It also seems fitting that this small effort should be produced in time to mark the centenary, in 1982, of the granting of the first patent to Obermaier, covering a package dyeing machine. Although hank processing may not be as important now, the opportunity has been taken to record much practical information which is currently or has been, in the recent past, widely known, but is in danger of becoming lost.

Although the opinions expressed and the errors are undoubtedly my own, appreciation must be expressed to my colleagues who have contributed considerably. Special mention must be made of Messrs T. M. Thompson and J. S. Mason who have produced much of the technical data on which the book is based. Many friends and colleagues in the industry have given useful help.

February 1981   J.P.

List of tables

TABLES

List of illustrations

Contents

CHAPTER 1

Introduction

With the possible exception of materials for certain industrial uses, most textiles are subjected to some form of coloration process, either dyeing or printing, during the manufacturing sequence. Colour is accepted as an everyday part of life and the addition of colour to textile substrates greatly adds to their value and their usefulness.

Dyeing can be carried out at several stages of the manufacturing sequence, as is shown in Figure 1.1 for both synthetic and natural fibres.

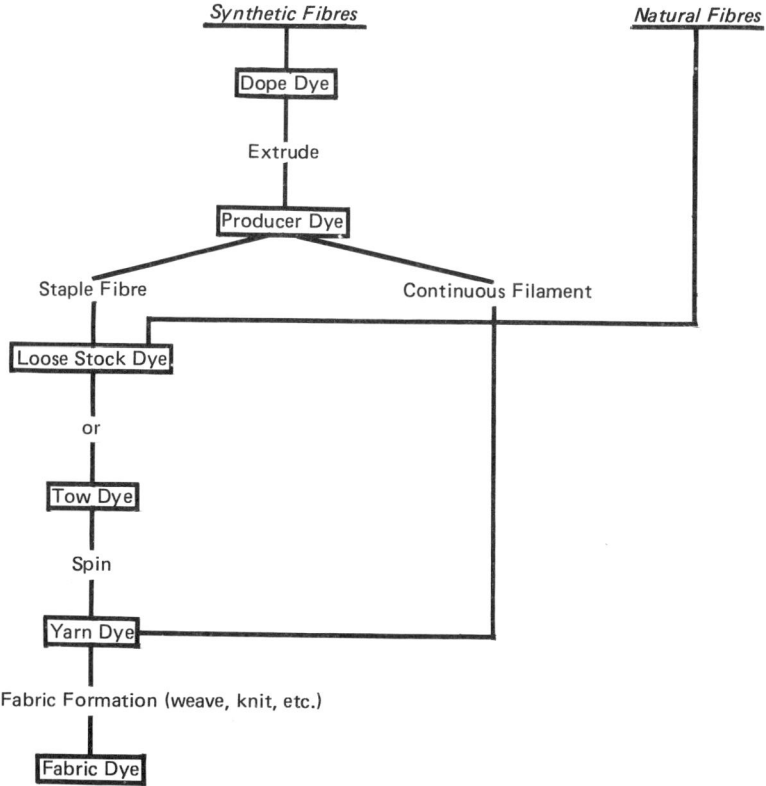

Figure 1.1 — Stages for dyeing

1

Carpet manufacture is a large and important sector of the textile industry, and Figure 1.2 shows the manufacturing sequence for carpets as well as the stages at which dyeing may take place.

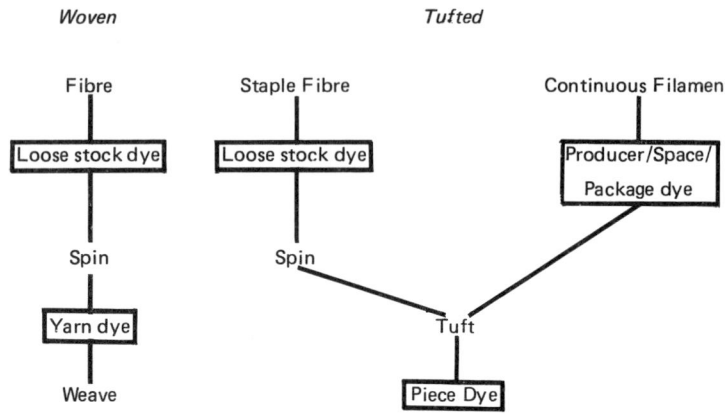

Figure 1.2 — Carpet routes

The latter is influenced by a number of factors. On economic grounds, dyeing early in the manufacturing sequence is the least costly. Dyeing at this stage also allows dyes possessing high fastness properties to be used, any unlevelness being corrected in subsequent spinning processes. Dyeing late in the manufacturing sequence gives economies due to the elimination of coloured waste and a reduction in the stock holding of coloured goods, since grey material can be dyed to suit the dictates of fashion. However, dye selection is more restricted since level results are more important, the nearer the dyeing process is to the delivery point.

Certain effects can only be produced by a specific route. For example, heather mixture effects, although possible via space dyeing, are generally produced by a fibre-dyeing process. On the other hand, dyeing in fabric form may be an intrinsic part of the total finishing sequence, as in the production of velours. In this case, dyeing is often preceded and followed by raising and brushing operations.

Yarn dyeing in general falls midway between many of these requirements in that level dyeings of high fastness can be obtained while allowing ecru, that is, undyed yarn, to be spun with the attendant economic advantage and shortened delivery time. The use of dyes of high fastness usually enables a high degree of reproducibility to be obtained.

1.1 COMPARISON OF YARN-DYEING PROCESSES

Many textile materials have been traditionally dyed in yarn form.
Hank and package dyeing methods can be summarized as follows:

Hank dyeing has the following characteristics:
— hank dyed yarn has a fuller bulk and handle
— tangling may occur
— hank reeling and back-winding is costly and may generate waste
— levelness may be inferior to package-dyed yarn
— the payload is less for a given machine size.

Package dyeing is characterized by the following:
— leaner yarn, but the yarn gives better fabric definition
— larger payloads for a machine of a given size
— faster back-winding and less waste generation
— high degrees of levelness and reproducibility, with the possibility of using dyes of high fastness
— savings in energy, water, etc., and space.

The traditional demarcation into materials which were hank or package dyed is given in Table 1.1.

TABLE 1.1

Product Categories

Hank	Package
Hand-knitting yarn	Singles cotton yarn
High-bulk acrylic	Singles yarn for marl yarns
Carpet yarn	Viscose cake
	Sewing thread
	Continuous filament yarn

1.2 THE BACKGROUND TO PACKAGE PROCESSING

This traditional categorization is gradually disappearing as technical means are being found to produce certain products that were considered satisfactory only if hank dyed. The advantages claimed for package dyeing over hank dyeing include the following:

— elimination of hank reeling
— reduction in waste
— faster back-winding speeds
— more controllable dyeing process with better levelness and the use of faster dyes
— savings in water, effluent, energy, dyes and chemicals due to the lower liquor ratio used
— less space required
— less labour handling
— more production from a machine of a given size
— high-temperature dyeing possible and rapid drying
— readily automated processes.

Criticisms of package dyeing have generally centred around the increased cost of plant and the fear that a less bulky yarn will result. This latter fear has been dismissed in many areas either by the modification of the process or a change in yarn specification. There have also been unfounded fears that fast dyes on shrink-resisted wool cannot produce level dyeings. Higher-twist weaving yarns, whether for solid shades or marl effects, are often dyed as singles and then twisted to ensure a level product. However, with current technology, it is doubtful if this precaution is necessary.

Currently, yarns of many fibre types for a large range of end-uses, can be package dyed successfully. The following list, while by no means exhaustive, is intended to give an indication of the products manufactured via this route:

Texturized yarns for both weaving and knitting
Sewing thread
Singles yarn for use as such or for the production of marl effects
Regular acrylic yarns for machine knitting or weaving
Weaving yarns in wool and acrylic fibres for apparel or furnishing
High-bulk acrylic yarns for machine knitting
Cellulosic yarns for weaving or machine knitting.

1.3 THE PHILOSOPHY AND CONCEPTS OF PACKAGE DYEING

A principal advantage of package dyeing is that, if it is considered as a total concept, it is amenable to a high level of control. Many of the factors contributing to this control will be detailed in subsequent sections, but it should be recognized that package dyeing is a high-technology process. The philosophy of package dyeing can be outlined briefly as follows:

— the production of a standard dye package, in terms of traverse, diameter, weight and density
— weighing and counting of these into dyelots
— the use of press-packing techniques, to give a uniform standard spindle density
— the use of dyeing machines of high design standards, including such features as wider spindle diameters and larger pump capacities
— use of dyeing machines at standard loadings to give reproducible liquor ratios
— characterization of dyeability of substrate
— rationalization of dye ranges to a small number per fibre and end use
— the use of standardized dyes
— the use of dyes of high fastness and reproducibility
— monitored/recorded weighing of dyes and chemicals
— dispensing facilities
— automation of total dyeing process, especially the time/temperature profile
— a high level of reproducibility from laboratory to bulk and between batches as a result of the above factors so that 'blind' dyeing techniques* can be used.

The use of this philosophy not only assists in achieving level results and the production of a high quality yarn but also gives maximum payloads with a high degree of reproducibility so that productivity and efficiency at a high level is obtained. Quality control procedures have been developed in which dyeing

*'Blind' dyeing techniques are those in which the dyeing cycle is carried to completion without any intermediate examination of the material for shade.

quality is assessed, particularly with blind dyeing techniques, while the yarn is still on the dyeing frame. Selected packages are knitted against the standard for both levelness and for shade assessment before the yarn proceeds to the next process.

A major disadvantage of package dyeing is that in many cases it introduces two additional winding operations into the total process route, with a subsequent increase in cost.

In 1969, Atkins [1] forecast a significant increase in the amount of package dyeing carried out in the wool industry. It was estimated that by the mid 1970s, package-dyed output would have increased by 100% with only 14% increase in hank dyeing. The production of piece-dyed materials, loose stock and top-dyed material would have been reduced by 7, 8 and 38%, respectively. The fact that these predictions have not been met may be due to two factors:

(i)   the high cost of purchasing and installing package-dyeing equipment, and

(ii)   the development of less costly producer dyeing and continuous tow dyeing processes.

Indeed, these latter coloration methods have already eroded the acrylic yarn dyeing market, by 1979 it had been reduced to 30% of the 1973 level.

1.4 THE BACKGROUND TO HANK PROCESSING

Whereas package dyeing dates back to around 1882, when the first patent was issued to Obermaier, hank dyeing has a much longer history and probably dates back to antiquity when yarn was simply suspended on wooden poles and turned by hand. This process has been in existence until fairly recently in some dyehouses, but because of the age of the process, development of machines has been longer and more complex than the corresponding development in package dyeing. The importance and popularity of hank dyeing relative to package dyeing can perhaps be gauged by the fact that, at the ITMA exhibition held in Hanover in 1979, only four machinery manufacturers showed hank-dyeing machines, compared to about twenty who were exhibiting package-dyeing machines.

Atkins [1] forecast a decrease in the importance of the hank-dyeing process, but the fact that these prophecies have not been entirely fulfilled is probably due to the following factors:

—   many spinners are still equipped with hank-reeling machines, as the last operation in the spinning process

—   the cost of shipping press-packed hanks, especially from the Far-East and particularly with acrylic yarns, is much less than for yarn on cone

—   there are still a large number of hank machines, albeit of dubious performance and life expectation, in operation.

—   the high cost of purchasing and installing more sophisticated machines in a time of economic recession has slowed down the disappearance of hank

—   the introduction of multi-purpose machines, which are able to dye hank as one of the options, has prolonged the life of the process

—   it is often claimed that, with certain products, a better quality is obtained by the hank route.

1.5 CHARACTERISTICS OF HANK DYEING

Hank dyeing is usually judged to give a yarn with a more fully developed bulk and a fuller handle than that obtained by package-dyeing routes. The same is often said when comparing hank dyed materials with those which have been produced by fibre dyeing methods. This is probably because the hanks, as suspended on the poles or sticks of the dyeing machine, are free to relax completely and are not constrained in any way. This not only allows for full bulk development but allows a certain freedom for twist in the yarn to run and find its equilibrium, thus removing spinning tensions.

In general, hank-dyeing machines are relatively simple and this can give economics in maintenance. The purchase price of simpler types is also relatively low when compared with that of more sophisticated machines. However, payloads are generally lower for a given size than for the corresponding package machine and much more floor space is required for hank handling, both in terms of machine space and for ancillary operations. The machines themselves may have a relatively low flow rate so that restrictions are often placed on the levelness which can be obtained and the standard of fastness properties which can be achieved. This is often fibre specific.

The process is labour intensive, since a great deal of handling is required, not only in loading and unloading the dyeing machines themselves but also in the associated processes. With a yarn that has to be scoured before dyeing, it may be handled up to eleven times between the end of the spinning line and being available as dyed yarn on cone, as indicated by Table 1.2.

TABLE 1.2

Handling of Yarn in Hank Form

Remove yarn from spinning or doubling frame
Hank reel
Load and unload from continuous hank-scouring machine
Load and unload from hank-dyeing machine
Load and unload from centrifuge
Load and unload from thermal dryer
Back-wind

A degree of skill is required for loading the yarn on to the dyeing frames, since this can have a serious effect on the quality of the dyed yarn produced. The number of hanks per pole must be determined and the same number placed on each one so that an even load is obtained. The hanks must be correctly placed or 'dressed' on the poles so that the yarn is opened out and any twists within the hank removed. Tangling of hanks may still occur during dyeing, and the care with which frames are unloaded may well determine whether or not an acceptable level of waste generation is obtained in subsequent rewinding.

Hank reeling and back-winding on to cone are costly processes and both can give significant quantities of waste yarn.

1.6 PRODUCTS FROM HANK DYEING

Certain products have been traditionally hank dyed because of the bulking characteristics imparted by the process. Hand-knitting yarns are almost exclusively dyed by this technique when yarn dyeing is undertaken to develop the full bulk potential. Even so, the highest quality products are still processed through a continuous relaxing machine of the Superba type, to ensure maximum bulk before the yarn is balled for sale. Much yarn for use in woven carpets has been traditionally hank dyed and the vast capacity that is available in that industry for such processing has virtually ensured that no alternative process can seriously compete.

Table 1.3 lists the products that are hank dyed. This is by no means intended to be exhaustive, but gives a general indication of the most important product areas.

TABLE 1.3

Products from Hank Dyeing

Hand-knitting yarns, in wool, nylon, acrylic and blends of these fibres
Regular carpet yarns in wool, wool/nylon, acrylic
High-bulk acrylic carpet yarns
High-twist carpet yarns for the production of 'kinky' carpets
Regular acrylic yarns for machine knitting
High-bulk acrylic yarns for machine knitting — bulking and dyeing at the same time

1.7 THE PHILOSOPHY OF HANK DYEING

Although the origins of hank dyeing are ancient, with the availability of modern hank-dyeing machines, which will be described in a later section, the process can be controlled to a high level. Since they have few pumps and valves requiring control, hank-dyeing machines are relatively simple to automate. The machine itself requires only controlled fill and drain valves, a level probe, a controlled circulation pump and a means of controlling the time/temperature profile.

Many of the details given later (see Section 4.1.7), regarding the automation and control of package dyeing machines and processes, are applicable to the hank process.

Providing that certain parameters are controlled, a high degree of reproducibility can be obtained, with consequent cost savings and quality improvements. No apology is given for re-stating the important factors, as regards hank dyeing, in Table 1.4.

This overall approach assists in achieving level results, the production of high quality yarn, gives a high degree of reproducibility with the ability to use blind-dyeing or no-addition techniques. Addition of dyes to correct the shade, as well as reprocessing in hank machines is less than satisfactory, since unlevel results are often obtained due to lower circulation efficiencies available. Quality control procedures have been developed in which dyeing quality, particularly with blind-dyeing techniques, is assessed while the yarn is still on the dyeing frame. Selected hanks, particularly from the four corners of rectangular dyeing frames,

TABLE 1.4

Important Control Parameters

Weighing of dyelots
Use of dyeing machines at standard loadings and liquor levels
Characterization of dyeability of substrate
Rationalization of dye ranges
Use of standardized dyes
Monitored/recorded weighing of dyes and auxiliaries
Dispensing facilities
Standard application techniques
Automated control, especially of time/temperature profiles
High level of laboratory-to-bulk and between-batch reproducibility

are knitted against the standard for both levelness and shade assessment before the yarn proceeds to the next stage. This is especially important in view of the labour required to unload and reload faulty dyeings.

In certain textile areas, notably Italy, hank dyeing appears to be much preferred, supposedly on quality grounds but perhaps somewhat influenced by low local labour costs. However, in Italy, hank processing has probably been developed further, from a machinery standpoint, than in other countries. Modern, sophisticated, hank-dyeing machines, with a high level of control equipment, including the continuous monitoring of dyebath exhaustion, are in use. Special handling systems (Chapter 3) have been developed, and even tumble drying of jumbo hanks is undertaken in an effort to achieve maximum bulk development in the yarn.

In general, yarn dyeing has the disadvantage that it is a more costly route than dyeing in the fibre form. However, it has the advantage that it is nearer to the point of delivery and, therefore can more readily take account of fashion changes in colours. Batch sizes can be smaller through this route and, in view of the current economic climate, few manufacturers can perhaps risk ordering the large weights per colour normally associated with the coloration processes nearer the beginning of the processing route, with the consequent cash flow problems.

REFERENCE

1. Atkins, *'The Strategic Future of the Wool Textile Industry'*, Wool Textile E.D.C. (1969).

CHAPTER 2

Package preparation

The success of package dyeing, in terms of both levelness and yarn quality, is greatly influenced by the degree of care taken in the preparation of the yarn packages. Useful information regarding package preparation has been given by Whittaker [1], who recognized the importance of uniform packages of a suitable package density. The density of the package may be controlled during the winding process by adjusting the yarn tension and the winding speed.

A wide range of designs and materials has been used as support media for packages; some of these will be discussed in greater detail in subsequent sections. A range of inserts, by no means exhaustive, used for both texturized and spun yarns, is illustrated in Figure 2.1.

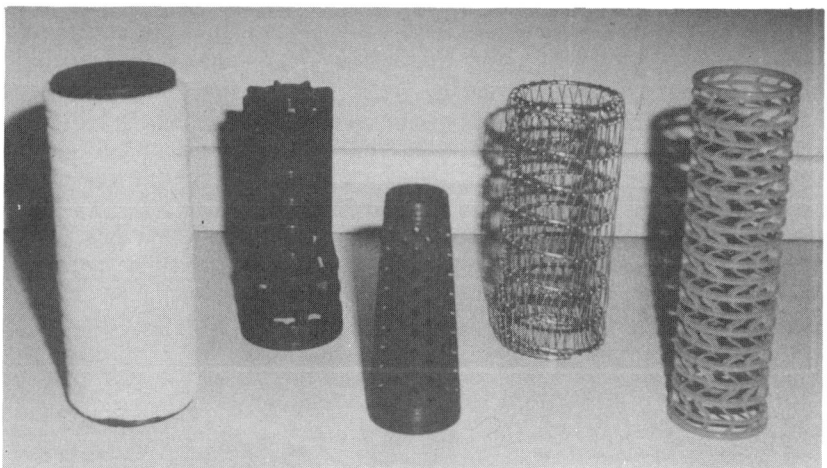

Figure 2.1 — Range of package centres

Rockets, cones, springs, plastic tubes and non-woven fabric centres have all found favour and will be discussed throughout this chapter. The patented Tigges springs have been widely used for dyeing high-bulk acrylic yarn, since they allow a certain amount of shrinkage to occur in the package due to compression of the spring in both width and length. As with most stainless steel formers, cost can be a serious problem, especially if a large number is required, due to their use in supply packages.

Both metal and plastic formers can be used and this is perhaps most widely recognized in the case of cones. Metal formers, although expensive, are obviously more robust, generally more durable and easy to clean. Plastic formers are less expensive, but have a shorter life and can be heavily stained by certain dyes, which can cause contamination problems.

Texturized yarns are frequently wrapped in stockinette for dyeing since this prevents filamentation of the yarn (i.e. separation and breaking of filaments) and helps to keep the yarn clean. Use of unsuitable stockinette material or prolonged recycling of these wrappers can cause problems due to staining.

2.1 TEXTURIZED YARNS

Texturized yarns are traditionally package dyed. Broadhurst [2] has described the technique whereby the packages are loaded into annular baskets, of the type used for dyeing loose stock, often using wet packing and stamping techniques, and a solid, wall-like mass of yarn is established. This method is the only one in which packages of varying size and density can be used. This technique, however, has now been replaced by the more conventional one of loading packages on to the spindles, either directly or using some form of insert.

Steel springs or plastic tubes may be used as inserts, but these can add considerably to the dyeing cost if used as a supply centre as opposed to an in-house package. Plastic centres can be expensive, especially if they can only be used once, such as the Aflex type, unless the dyeing package can be used, without rewinding, as the supply package for warping, weaving or knitting. An alternative method is to prepare yarn on to a push-out cardboard former from which the packages are loaded directly on to the spindles.

The main advantage of all packages for texturized yarn is that they are prepared on the texturizing machine, thereby eliminating a winding process. A typical package specification for texturized yarn is given in Table 2.1.

TABLE 2.1

Package Specification for Texturized Yarn

Package weight	1 kg
Package diameter	220 mm
Package centre diameter	56 mm
Package traverse length	140 mm
Angle of traverse wind	15° 40′
Package density	220 g/l
Spindle density of packages after press-packing on column	280 g/l

As will be mentioned again later, press packing is an integral stage in processing parallel-sided packages since it gives a uniform spindle density as well as minimizing any slight differences in package density.

2.2 STAPLE YARNS

Staple yarns have conventionally been delivered to the package dyer on perforated cones ready for dyeing. The conicity of the cone is usually $4°20'$ or $5°57'$. This method has the advantage that a winding process is eliminated, but the dyer has little control over the package densities produced. Furthermore, expensive spacing devices are required and, even with these, cones can slip on the dyeing machine spindle giving rise to liquor channelling and the risk of unlevel dyeing. The payload with cones is less than that with other forms of package, and cone rounding is usually necessary to remove hard shoulders. Dyeing on cone can limit the use of certain handling and drying methods; these will be discussed later. However, much yarn is dyed on cone satisfactorily, but the use of cones is perhaps best limited to small cones and lower payloads in vertical (in-house) operations. Cone-dyeing of cotton has been widely practised.

An alternative to cone dyeing is to dye on a Delerue rocket package. In this method, the rocket winder uses a principle whereby the yarn traverses from the inside to the outside of the package over a distance of approximately 18 inches, which tends to mask the effect of any unlevel dyeing. This method has not been widely used but has been discussed in detail [3] and the method of winding is shown in Figure 2.2.

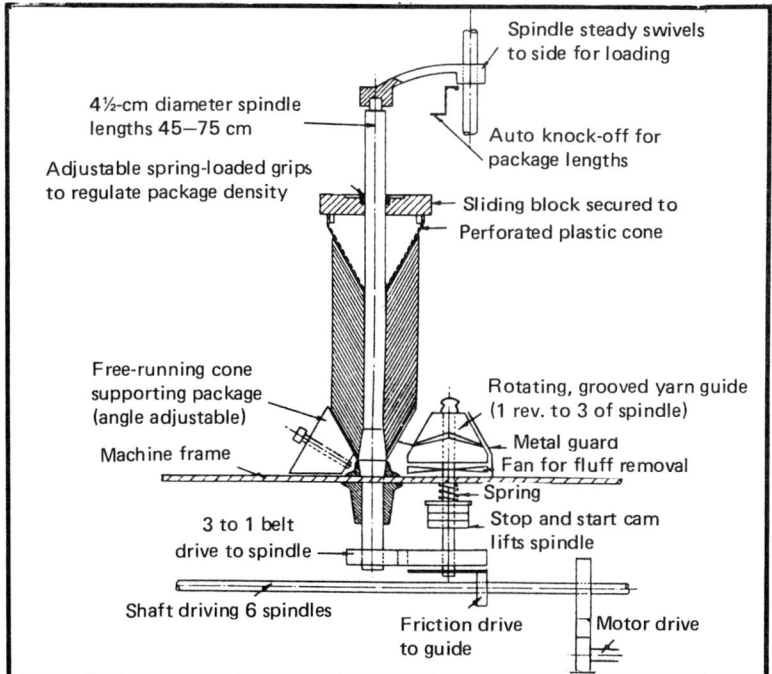

Figure 2.2 – Rocket winding

Denton [4] has shown that parallel-sided packages are preferable because of their better liquor flow characteristics. Soft-wound packages should be avoided, since dye-liquor channelling can occur due to package distortion, preventing direct use of the packages, because they become unsuitable for subsequent twisting, in the case of singles yarn, or to feed fabric-forming machinery. Stable, high density packages are preferable since they can be used without rewinding, while increased package sizes allied to press packing, which levels out variations between packages, gives increased dyelot sizes and at the same time level dyeing.

Regular, staple yarn is rewound from the supply package which may be a cone or cardboard tube. Many winding machines are suitable, such as the Fadis TUAN—F or TU.RO/F, which is illustrated diagramatically in Figure 2.3. Winding speeds up to 1300 m/min are claimed.

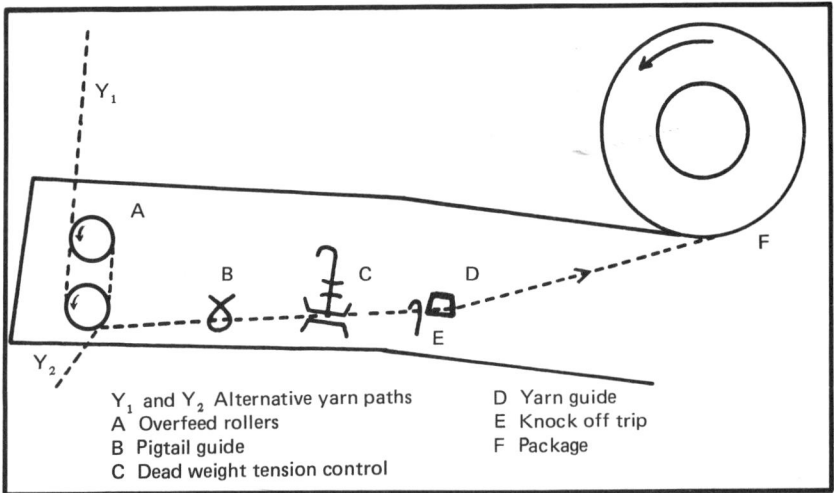

Y_1 and Y_2 Alternative yarn paths   D Yarn guide
A Overfeed rollers   E Knock off trip
B Pigtail guide   F Package
C Dead weight tension control

Figure 2.3 — Fadis TUAN—F winding machine

The winding machine should be provided with a mandrel of the same diameter as the spindle on the dyeing machine so that packages can be prepared using polypropylene non-woven centres of either a re-usable or throw-away variety. The mandrel functions as the push-out centre on which the package is transported to the loading area. This technique can be used satisfactorily for most fibre types and end-uses and a typical package specification is shown in Table 2.2.

With the development of spinning techniques, such as open-end methods, it is possible to prepare dyeing packages directly from the spinning frame. In addition, parallel-sided packages can be prepared directly from the two-for-one twister such as Volkmann. Both of these developments make it possible to produce parallel-sided packages to the specification given below, while eliminating a winding process.

TABLE 2.2

Specification for Staple Yarns

Package weight	1.5 kg
Package diameter	220 mm
Package centre diameter	69 to 72 mm
Package traverse	190 mm
Angle of traverse wind	12°
Package density	200 g/l
Spindle density of packages after press-packing on column	260 g/l

2.3 BI—KO

A recent advance (1979) has been the development of the BI—KO centre by Rost [5]. These are biconical formers made of polypropylene, later versions being reinforced with glass fibre to withstand dyeing temperatures up to 140°C. The internal geometry of the former is 4°20' which means that many conventional cone-winding machines can be used to prepare the parallel-sided packages. Grooves in the base of the formers correspond with vanes in the top so that press packing techniques can be used. These formers are illustrated in Figure 2.4.

Figure 2.4 — BI—KO formers

This development gives the advantages of press-packing associated with parallel-sided packages without the disadvantages of cones, while allowing the spinner to prepare the dyeing packages, thus eliminating a winding process, if these can be supplied to an appropriate specification. Such a specification is given in Table 2.3 and comparisons are given in this table with cone and parallel-sided dyepacks, all prepared to a package weight of 1.3 kg.

TABLE 2.3

BI–KO Compared with Other Package Types

	Cone	BI–KO	Parallel-sided
Package density (g/l)	350	335	340
Spindle density (g/l)	—	375	405
Number of packages/spindle	5	7	9
Weight of yarn/spindle (kg)	6.5	9.1	11.7

2.4 HIGH-BULK ACRYLIC YARNS

Preparation of high-bulk yarn packages by the dyer is justified since the continuous relaxation of the yarn is carried out at the same time.

High-bulk acrylic yarns were conventionally dyed in hank form to allow for approximately 20% shrinkage which occurs due to the relaxation of the yarn in water at about $85°C$ (and above).

Various machines have been developed for the continuous relaxation of the yarn using steam or dry heat. The principle of the operation is to unwind the unrelaxed yarn from cones through the relaxation chamber, the yarn then being wound on to suitable packages for dyeing. Attention must be paid to the package size and density which is influenced by the take-up tension. Available machines of this type are listed in Table 2.4.

The main methods used commercially are:

(i)   the stuffer box / 'J'-tube technique developed by Hacoba
(ii) the conveyor belt method of Superba
(iii) the conveyor band, originally developed by Hörauf Sussen and now expanded by Savio

TABLE 2.4

Continuous Relaxation Machines

System	Model	Bulking Media	Technique
ARTC	Metier 2020/07 HB27	Hot air	
Hacoba	HB	Saturated or superheated steam	Stuffer box
Hörauf	CVA	Saturated steam or hot air	Conveyor band
Hirschburger	HBS	"	"
Savio	RRS	"	"
Superba	Spirovac	Saturated steam	Conveyor belt

All the machines listed undoubtedly produce satisfactory yarn, but the choice of machine may depend on a number of factors; these are listed in Table 2.5.

TABLE 2.5

Factors in Continuous Bulking Machines

Space required
Output required
Package size and traverse
Cost
Reliability
Availability of spares
Sophistication of uptake winder
Residual shrinkage
Labour content (i.e. no. of ends/operative)

The Hacoba, with its sophisticated Fadis back-winding unit, and the Superba are widely-used machines and these are shown diagrammatically in Figures 2.5 and 2.6.

The preparation of packages on polypropylene centres is carried out as described earlier.

In preparing packages of high bulk acrylic yarn for dyeing, the feeding-on tension of the yarn and the force existing between the driving barrel and the winding package must be adjusted to achieve two primary targets: to produce a yarn with an elliptical cross-section, as opposed to a flat-ribbon type yarn, as laid on the package; and to obtain a package of even density throughout. A perfectly vertical, flush edge is required on the package so that adjacent packages bed down together on spindles.

2.5 CARPET YARNS

Staple carpet yarns can be package dyed, since the yarn can be wound onto dye packages from spinner's or doubler's tubes, thereby eliminating a winding operation. Winding can be carried out on the Fadis type of machine as described earlier to give packages of 1 to 1.5 kg.

Continuous filament yarn can be handled on springs which are prepared by the fibre producer. Alternatively, both types of yarn can be wound into dye packages using the Gilbos GR 10R machine, to give packages with a traverse of 200—260 mm weighing up to 5 kg. These packages are ideally suited for direct tufting.

2.6 KNIT—DEKNIT (KDK) YARN

Continuous filament yarn for the production of 'crinkle' type fabrics is knitted into tubular fabric approximately 8 cm in diameter. Rolls of this fabric can be handled as dye packages on spindle machines and after wet processing are deknitted. This type of package is handled in essentially the same way as the others.

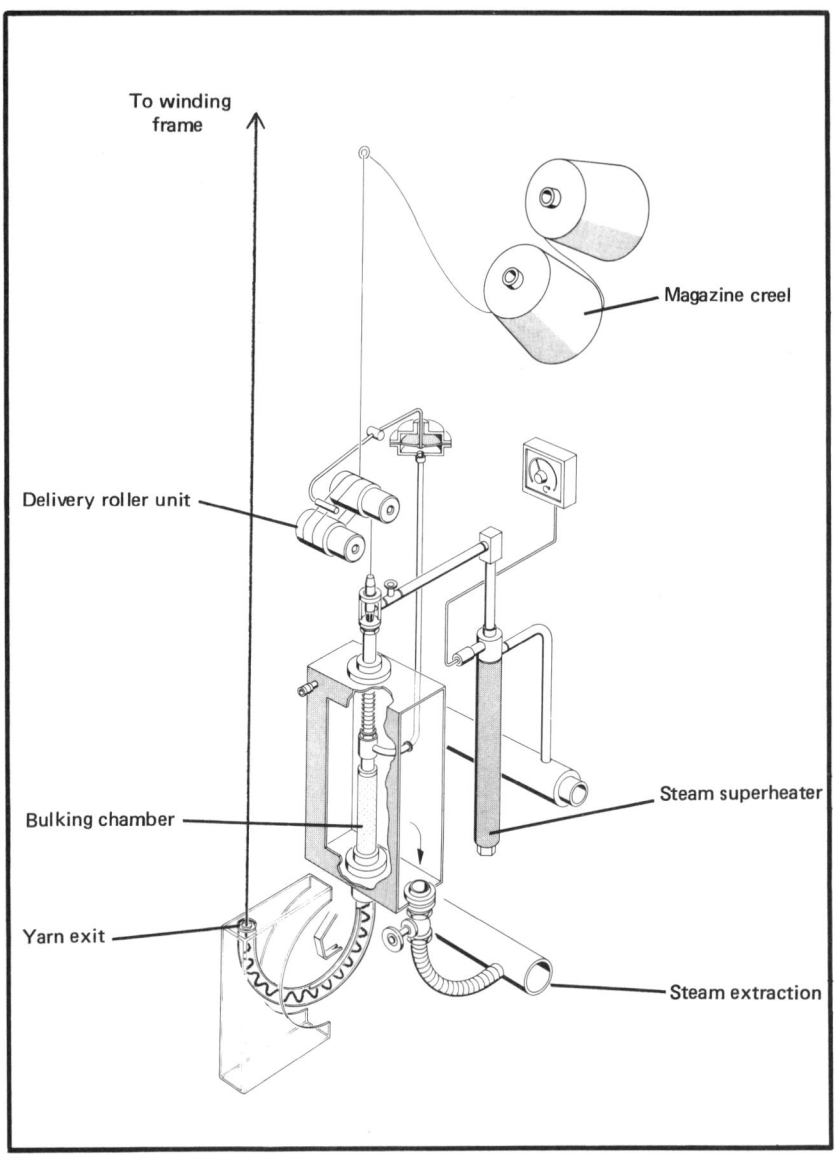

Figure 2.5 — Principle of Hacoba unit

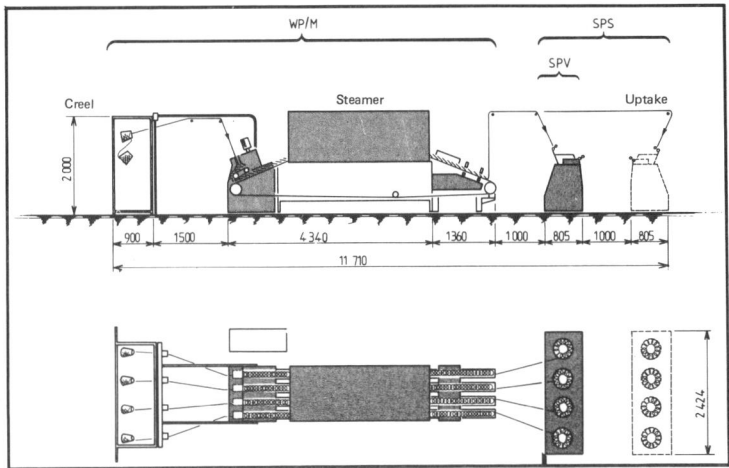

Figure 2.6 — Principle of Superba Spirovac unit

2.7 PRESS PACKING

Several references have already been made to the philosophy of press packing, in which dye packages are prepared to a given specification. The packages are loaded manually on to the dyeing spindles then additional packages are loaded by means of a mechanical press giving a package compression of 25 to 40%. This technique, in addition to giving increased payloads minimizes package density differences, prevents liquor channelling and contributes greatly to level dyeing. Column or spindle density is thus a most important factor. A typical package press is illustrated in Figure 2.7.

When the packages have been press packed, a smooth vertical, column of yarn is produced in which any variation in package preparation can be readily seen.

2.8 PREPARATION FOR DYEING

Scouring is not readily carried out in package dyeing machines, largely due to the filtration effects produced by the yarns. Thus, excessively dirty yarns can cause problems in package dyeing and most yarns are either dry spun or are spun with a self-scouring, water-soluble or emulsifiable lubricant which can be removed by water rinsing only, or will be stable in the dyebath during dyeing.

It may be necessary to give some synthetic-fibre yarns a light scour in the machine before dyeing to remove certain spin finish residues, etc. Soxhlet extraction of a yarn sample with solvents, such as methylene chloride, is carried out before and after scouring to determine the level of extractable matter. After scouring these values should be 0.5% or less and it is important that any extractable material on the yarn is evenly distributed, otherwise this can cause unlevel dyeing. Heavy deposits on the inside of the package can cause serious problems,

Figure 2.7 — Package press

and to minimize this, scouring and rinsing should be carried out on two-way flow.

REFERENCES

1. Whittaker, *J.S.D.C.*, **77** (1961) 690.
2. Broadhurst, in *'The Dyeing of Synthetic-polymer and Acetate Fibres'*, ed. D. M. Nunn, (Bradford: Dyers Company Publications Trust, 1979) 201.
3. Jowett, *Dyer,* **138** (1967) 585.
4. Denton, *J. Textile Inst.,* **54** (1963) T406.
5. Rost, Patent applied for.

CHAPTER 3

Hank preparation

Following spinning and doubling, the yarns are reeled into hanks on hank-reeling machines which are fitted with swifts having a circumference of approximately 120–230 cm. The length of hank produced is influenced by the section of the industry being supplied and it is important that the length of hank produced at reeling can be accommodated in the dyeing machines and on the swifts of subsequent back-winding machines. Thus, thought must be given to the length of frames and depth of hank-dyeing machines relative to the hank type being produced. In the case of high-bulk yarns, which will shrink 18 to 25% during dyeing, due allowance must be made for this change in length. Currently, the average length of hank produced is usually within the range 140–180 cm.

Conventionally, hank weights are approximately in the range 340 to 450 g and these were fastened at various places around the hank with tie-bands to preserve the integrity of the hank and prevent tangling. Tie-bands which are too tight will give rise to undyed places in the hank. Recent developments have centred on the use of so-called 'jumbo' hanks which can be as large as 2 kg for hosiery and up to 10 kg for carpet yarns.

In one such system, developed by Fadis, the tie-bands are dispensed with and the hanks are wrapped in heat-set polyester stockinette which protects the yarn throughout processing and prevents yarn entanglement. The claims made for the use of jumbo hank processing include:

- up to 30% increase in capacity of the dyeing machine
- better yarn quality and less entanglement
- less waste
- increased efficiency in back-winding with machine efficiencies up to 95%
- fewer knots
- back-winding at faster speeds with less labour
- because of increased machine loading, considerable savings in dyes, chemicals, labour, water, effluent and energy.

Indeed, the processing of jumbo hanks, particularly in the carpet industry, has achieved in whole or in part many of the advantages claimed for package dyeing and has resulted in reduced interest in package-dyeing methods. This is further the case since the introduction of jumbo hank processing requires only a minimum capital expenditure in the winding plant and no investment at all in the dyehouse. In large-size jumbo hanks, considerable tensions and strains can be set up in individual threads of the hank during reeling. It is recommended that tumbling be carried out before dyeing such hanks, in order to remove such tensions. Failure to do so can result in unlevel dyeing as evidenced by stripes in the fabric produced.

Reeling of hanks ready for dyeing is exclusively carried out by the spinner and is not undertaken by the dyer, contrary to the practice for package dyeing. Manufacturers of hank-reeling machines include those listed in Table 3.1.

TABLE 3.1

Manufacturers of Hank-reeling Machines

Company	Address
Croon and Lucke	Stuttgart, W. Germany
Delerue	Roubaix, France
Eadie Bros Ltd	Manchester, England
Monocono	Tarrasa, Barcelona, Spain
Nestel	Reutlingen, W. Germany
Rof	Sabadell, Barcelona, Spain
SACM	Mulhouse, France
SIMA	Bologna, Italy
Socomat	Florence, Italy
SWA	Biella, Vercelli, Italy
Wilson & Longbottom Ltd	Barnsley, England
Zerbo	Brusnengo, Italy

3.1 HANK PROCESSES PRIOR TO DYEING

Many synthetic fibre yarns, particularly acrylic and also wool, are dry spun with only a small quantity (around 0.2%) of fibre lubricant or spinning assistant. These yarns require no scouring prior to dyeing. Others may receive only a rinse in water in the dyeing machine prior to dyeing. A treatment at $70°C$ for 15 minutes will be sufficient. Alternatively, a more severe scour for what are essentially clean yarns can be given in the dyeing machine using alkaline detergent such as:

> 3% Sufatol LS3 (Standard Chemicals)
> 3% Soda ash

for 20 minutes at $65°C$, followed by rinsing.

One advantage of hank processing is that yarns can be scoured in specially designed continuous scouring machines so that yarns heavily contaminated with spinning oil or dirt can be efficiently scoured.

3.2 COTTON YARNS

Yarn in hank form is processed in a similar fashion to fabric in that kier boiling and bleaching is carried out in enclosed vessels. Following this process, mercerization may be carried out in special machines, such as that illustrated in Figure 3.1. The hanks are placed over arms which apply tension. The arms also rotate and the yarn is immersed in a 350 g/l solution of sodium hydroxide (60°Tw or ca 27% NaOH by weight). The alkali is washed out while the hanks are still under tension, tension is then removed and the hanks finally rinsed in a dilute solution of acetic acid.

Figure 3.1 — Hank mercerizing machine

3.3 CONTINUOUS HANK SCOURING

Woollen and worsted yarns, unless dry spun, contain significant amounts of lubricating oil and are usually scoured in hank form in a continuous scouring machine. These machines are of two principal types, namely, brattice and tape machines. In the former, the yarn is carried through the scouring liquors between metal brattices, whereas in the latter, the yarn is carried between tapes. A scouring range is usually made up of three or four scouring troughs or bowls with a pair of squeeze rollers between each bowl. The top roller is usually lapped with wool or cotton sliver and the bottom roller is metal. Several tons pressure is usually applied by these rollers giving an expression of as low as 60%.

The principles of brattice and tape scouring machines are shown in Figures 3.2 and 3.3, respectively, and one bowl of the former type is illustrated in Figure 3.4.

The features of the two types of machine are summarized in Table 3.2.

TABLE 3.2

Characteristics of Scouring Machines

	Brattice	Tape
Length of bowls (m)	2.5–4	1.5–3.5
Width of bowls (cm)	80–135	70–120
Depth of bowls (cm)	55–85	55–85
Capacity (l)	1600–2500	500–2200
Running speed (m/min)	4.5	9

Due to the lower running speed, brattice machines give longer immersion times compared to the 6 to 12 seconds given by tape machines. With a loading of 0.5 kg of yarn per metre of tape, an output of 270 kg per hour can be obtained from a tape machine. Although a higher manning level is required, it has been possible to run at 1.5 kg of yarn per metre of tape with a production rate of 800 kg per hour. A comparison of production capacities of brattice machines is given in Table 3.3.

TABLE 3.3

Production from Brattice Machines

Machine width (cm)	Bowl Capacity (l)	Production (kg/h) Hosiery Yarn	Carpet Yarn
80	1700	200	320
120	2500	400	640

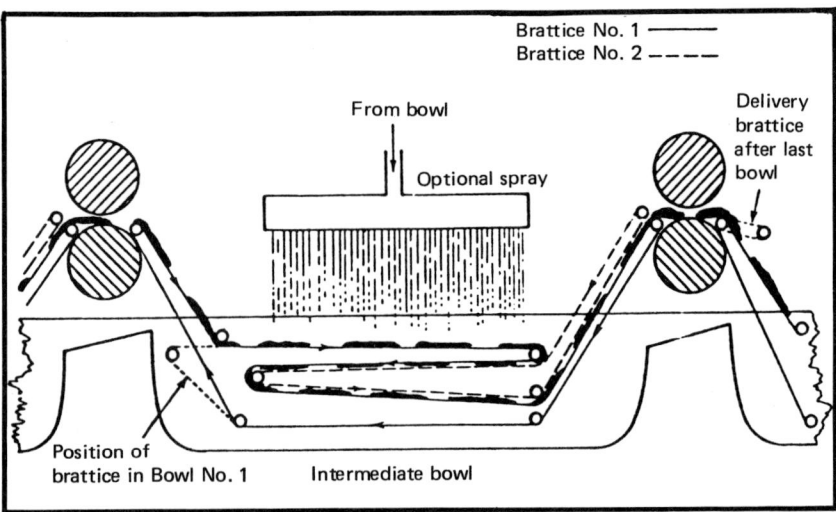

Figure 3.2 – Principle of a brattice scouring machine

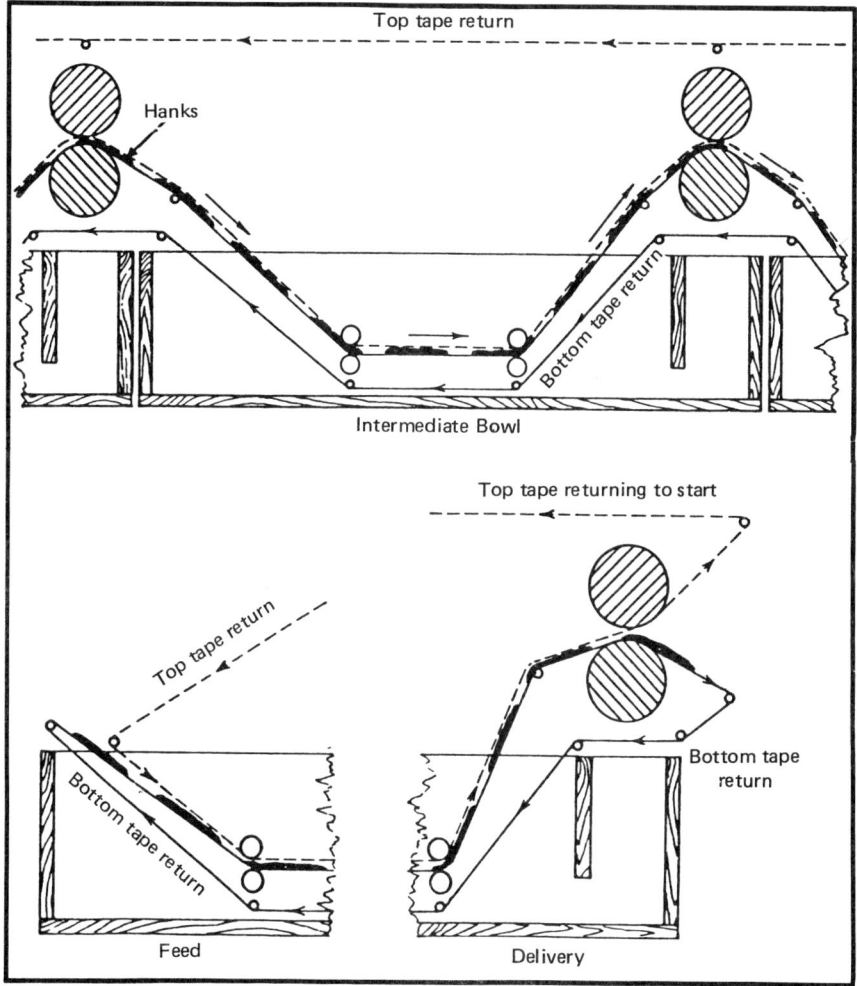

Figure 3.3 — Principle of a tape scouring machine

The bowls are usually heated by injecting direct steam through perforated pipes and the more modern machines have controlled steam valves to maintain the temperature at the desired level.

Woollen yarns are normally spun with a saponifiable oil, such as oleine, and although large quantities are employed — ranging from 5 to 15% on the weight of fibre — removal is relatively simple. Soda ash alone will form soap with the oil in situ, and this exerts a strong emulsifying action to remove the associated wool grease and dirt. Worsted yarns are spun with up to 3% of an emulsifiable

Figure 3.4 — One bowl of a brattice scouring machine

oil, this being removed by soap added to the scouring bath together with alkali as a soap builder and to adjust the pH, since acidic conditions in scouring should be avoided. Alternatively, alkaline solutions of synthetic detergents can be used. The make-up of typical scouring baths is shown in Table 3.4 together with the additions required as processing proceeds.

Due to the squeezing action obtained, hank processing can deal with much dirtier and oilier yarns, with a wider range of lubricant types, than package processing. Scouring ranges can also be used to rectify certain problems, such as

TABLE 3.4

Scouring Bath Make-up

Yarn Type	Bowl 1 Start	Bowl 1 Addition per 50 kg wool	Bowl 2 Start	Bowl 2 Addition per 50 kg wool	Bowl 3
Woollen					
Soda ash	3.5	2.8	1.0	1.1	Water only
Soap	0.1	—	0.05	—	
Temperature (°C)	60		50		40
Worsted					
Soap	0.1	0.2	—	—	Water only
Soda ash	0.2	0.9	—	—	
Non-ionic detergent	—	—	0.25	0.2	
Temperature (°C)	55		50		40

the unlevel application of soft finish, dirt marks, etc. The last bowl can be used to apply soft finishes to acrylic yarns after dyeing. Soft water should be used for scouring. Residual solvent-extractable matter should be below 0.5%.

3.4 WET SETTING OF WOOL YARNS

Certain yarns, such as those from crossbred wools, are wet set before scouring and hank dyeing to prevent cockling occurring in the piece. This process is carried out by stretching the hanks tightly between the sticks of a frame which is then immersed in boiling water for 30 minutes, the hanks being turned at least once throughout the process. The hanks are allowed to cool under tension, before removing from the frame.

The Klauder—Weldon machine, which will be discussed more fully later, was ideal for this process, because the hanks were turned continuously during the process. Since this machine has become obsolete, specially constructed stainless steel frames are fitted in conventional dyeing vessels.

It has also been shown, in previously unpublished work, that wet setting can prevent loss in strength with certain yarns in subsequent processing. This work was carried out on several yarns, but the results shown in Table 3.5 for singles yarn strength tests and elongation at break for 2/30's worsted yarn are typical.

TABLE 3.5

Effect of Processing on Yarn Strength

Yarn Details	Strength (g)	Extension at Break (%)
Ecru yarn in oil	360	15.0
Set with yarn held straight only	309	11.9
Set with yarn extended 2.5%	326	13.0
Set with yarn extended 5.0%	383	17.6
Set with yarn extended 5.0%, scoured	347	10.6
Set with yarn extended 5.0%, scoured and dyed	346	13.3
Scoured and dyed without setting	191	6.9

CHAPTER 4

Services and machinery

4.1 PACKAGE PROCESSING

4.1.1 Water

In common with all other types of dyeing and finishing plants, the package dyehouse requires a sufficient supply of water of suitable quality. This is needed both for processing and for cooling, since, with most package-dyeing machines, the exhausted dye-liquors are cooled by means of closed coils before discharge to waste. An additional requirement for the water used in the package dyehouse is a low suspended solids content, since packages act as ideal filters for such material.

It is usual practice to soften the water before use, and filtration may also be carried out at this stage. There are conflicting opinions as to the specification required for process water in the textile industry, but an example of such a specification for package dyeing is given in Table 4.1. The presence of metal ions in the water supply, or the addition of sequestering agents, such as ethylene-diamine tetra-acetic acid (EDTA), to the dye-liquor to combat such contaminants, can result in considerable colour changes with certain dyes. The effect on disperse dyes is well known, with C.I. Disperse Red 60 being an outstanding example.

TABLE 4.1

Process Water Specification

Colour (Hazen)	2–5	(clear)
Hardness (mg/l CaCO$_3$)	5	
Turbidity (FTU)	1	
Iron (Fe, mg/l)	0.01	
Copper (Cu, mg/l)	0.01	
Manganese (Mn, mg/l)	0.01	
Dissolved solids (mg/l)	250	
Suspended solids (mg/l)	5 or less	
pH	7 $\pm$ 1	

In conventional package-dyeing machines, the amount of water used for dyeing is quite small, since liquor-to-goods ratios of 8:1 are readily achieved by the use of press-packing techniques. In low-liquor machines, the liquor-to-goods ratio can be as low as 3:1.

In a modern package dyehouse, two to four times as much water is required for cooling purposes as is required for the actual dyeing process. This means that much more cooling water is produced than can be used directly for preparing dyebaths and this problem increases with the development of lower-liquor-ratio systems. In addition, unless high-temperature drains are used when dyeing polyester at temperatures of $130°C$, apart from the first few minutes of cooling, only low-grade hot water is obtained from the cooling-water return system. Where there are a number of machines, each at different stages of the cooling cycle at the same time, low-grade hot water may be obtained all the time. Furthermore, this water is too hot (about $35°C$) for return to the cold-water supply and, if this were done, two different supplies of warm water would result, neither of them suitable for hot or cold uses.

A higher grade of hot water can be obtained by slowing down the rate of flow of water in the cooling coils. This may increase cooling times to the extent that it cancels out the saving obtained at the beginning of the dyeing cycle due to the availability of hot water. A heating coil can also be installed in the hot-water tank, but, if all cooling water is returned to this tank, energy will be wasted in the hot water overflowing to drain. If all the cooling water is recycled, the effluent disposal cost may be reduced owing to a reduction in volume, but this can be off-set by an increase in cost owing to an increase in concentration. To enable all cooling water to be returned to the cold supply might result in considerable expense in the provision of a cooler.

One solution is to insert a level probe in the hot-water tank and a temperature probe in the cooling-water return which are both coupled, either electrically, pneumatically (to actuated valves), or controlled by means of a microprocesser. The sequence of events is then as follows: high-grade hot water, above a given temperature, is returned to the hot-water tank and heated by the heating coil to the required temperature to provide high-grade hot water to the dyehouse. Water much below the given temperature is returned to the cold-water supply. Water between the two temperatures is run to waste, except when the level in the hot-water tank is below a given level. In this case it is used to top up the tank and heated.

In view of the fact that water will always be running to waste and that only 10% is required for topping-up purposes when dyebaths can be recycled, some studies of dyebath recycling are apparently only of academic interest. The return of cooling water indiscriminately is ill-advised and careful feasibility studies should be undertaken before capital is spent on a costly recycling system.

It is obviously beneficial to recover a large proportion of cooling water to save heat, effluent, softening costs, etc. It has been found that, with a dyehouse using press-packing and operating at a liquor ratio of 12:1, the total water consumption (including cooling water) is 60 l per kg of yarn, even when a significant proportion of cooling water is recycled.

4.1.2 Effluent

With the increasing charges imposed by the water authorities for accepting dye-house effluent for treatment, added to the increasing pressures of legislation, there is undoubtedly a trend for dyehouses to carry out some effluent treatment. This may be restricted to simple balancing and sedimentation procedures, but such treatment is likely to be mandatory for a new operation. With old-established dyehouses, most of the effluents are accepted by the water autho-rities, since many of these operations are on sites where space is not available for the installation of an effluent treatment plant.

Where synthetic fibres are dyed and where scouring is limited, such as in the package-dyeing process, the effluent may in any case be relatively innocuous. Furthermore, liquor from package dyeing, if it has already been cooled, is not too hot for disposal. High alkalinities, such as those associated with scouring natural fibres or "reduction-clearing" of polyester fibres, and high-solids cont-ents, associated with scouring highly contaminated materials, may cause dif-ficulty. In such cases, some pre-treatment of the effluent is unavoidable.

Even where the effluent is accepted into the water authority sewers, certain conditions must be met; such a consent specification is shown in Table 4.2. Restrictions are also usually imposed on the volume of effluent which can be accepted per hour or per 24-hour period so that a flow meter is essential to record average and peak discharges.

TABLE 4.2

Consent Conditions for Effluent (Severn—Trent Water Authority)

Temperature	not above 43° C
pH	6—11
Suspended solids	400 mg/l
Chemical Oxygen Demand	800 mg/l

Soluble salts of chromium, copper, nickel, zinc, cadmium, tin and lead shall not exceed a total of *nil* mg/l

Total of insoluble and soluble compounds of chromium, copper, nickel, zinc, cadmium tin and lead shall not exceed *nil* mg/l

Cyanide, excluding ferrocyanide, shall not exceed *400* mg/l

Much useful information on many aspects of water and effluent has been given by Little [1].

4.1.3 Steam

An adequate supply of process steam is essential; the actual amount required will depend on the number of machines installed, their size and certain other factors, such as the desired rate of temperature rise. This last point requires careful consideration, if rapid-dyeing techniques, with high rates of temperature rise, are to be employed. It is usual to generate steam at a pressure of $7-8.5$ kg/cm^2, and to supply this throughout the factory by means of a $15-20$ cm ring main from which branches are taken off at appropriate points to service machines.

Nowadays, steam is usually generated by means of the "package" type of boiler plant, and this can be fired by either oil or natural gas. Dual firing is also possible, the method chosen depending largely on the economics of fuel supply at any given point in time. If natural gas is chosen as the main fuel, the gas-supply industry usually insists that this is liable to a three-month period of interruption since domestic users have first priority. This means that storage capacity for three months supply of oil is usually mandatory. Since this oil is not purchased on a regular basis, high prices may be paid and the storage life of the oil usually means that it must be used within a given period. Government has also tended to peg the price of alternative fuels to that of coal, so that the choice of the firing method for steam raising is indeed a complex one.

4.1.4 Compressed Air

Package-dyeing machines are controlled and operated by means of a large number of valves. Even if total automation is not employed, the valves are usually controlled from a local panel. Valves are usually activated by compressed air at well-regulated and defined pressures. Compressed air may also be used for lid seals.

An adequate supply of clean, dry, compressed air is thus essential and this is usually generated at 7 kg/cm^2 and reduced to the desired pressure at the valve according to requirements.

4.1.5 Pipework

It will be appreciated that considerable pipework is required for each dyeing machine and this is often hung at a high level on a pipe bridge to allow each pipe to descend to the necessary valve, etc. Services required include hot and cold water, steam line, condensate return, cooling-water supply and return, compressed air. Machine drains are often led into a common effluent drain.

As has been mentioned already, with respect to water and effluent discharge, every opportunity should be taken to save it. Pipes should be lagged to minimize energy consumption.

4.1.6 Plant layout

The layout of the plant should be such that work flow is unrestricted and bottle-necks are avoided. Adequate space for work in progress is required and attempts should be made to have a one-way flow arrangement without cross-over points. The space required is approximately 1000 to 1500 square feet per tonne of weekly production, if preparation, dyeing and back-winding are being carried out. For the plant as a whole, the traditional 'U'-shaped arrangement can fulfil the above requirements and a suggested general layout is shown in Figure 4.1.

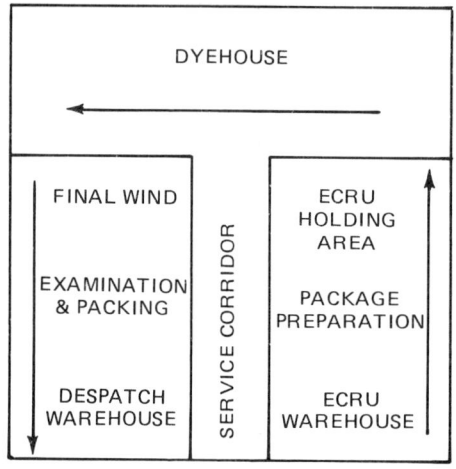

Figure 4.1 — Plant layout

In the dyehouse itself, the use of a three-tier system has been widely advocated, with ready access to pumps and services which are situated below the machine hall. The top tier houses the dispensary together with the control office and, perhaps, the laboratory. Whether or not automation is installed, the incorporation of a dispensary with mixing facilities which are remote from the dyehouse greatly contributes to the efficiency and cleanliness of the operations.

Prepared solutions of dyes and chemicals are fed from the dispensing tank to machines through glass piping. This relieves dyehouse operatives of all tasks except loading, unloading and taking samples.

In the colour dispensary, attention should be paid to the working environment so that steam, dust, etc., are removed for the benefit of operatives and to avoid contamination of dyes by water vapour or dust.

A lift is necessary to stores above ground level, and floors should be made of a chemically-resistant material of sufficient weight-carrying capacity. The area should be divided into dry weighing and wet dissolving sections. Thought should be given to suitable storage bays or racks for dyes and chemicals, but this is not made easy by the wide variations in size of package offered by manufacturers.

Adequate consideration must be given to handling devices such as cranes.

Totally enclosed machines, such as package-dyeing equipment, do not vent large quantities of steam into the atmosphere and thus the working environment is usually wholesome. In modern premises, air conditioning is usually installed and a controlled atmosphere is essential in instrument/computer rooms.

4.1.7 Automation

The use of automation in the control of dyeing operations is now well established. Although computer control of dyeing processes was originally conceived in order to achieve technical objectives, automation now contributes largely to the commercial or economic success of the operation since it is one method of combating the ever-increasing effects of inflation and general rising costs. Automation of dyeing processes has been well documented, including the description of many installations, and this large volume of literature has been reviewed recently [2].

The historical steps in the development of control can be briefly outlined as follows:

1. By the use of suitable activators, manually controlled functions can be controlled by switches centralized on a local panel
2. The use of a sequence controller on the local panel to control a complete cycle
3. The control of a dyeing machine by a logic system
4. The control of a number of machines, using a computer
5. The control of a dyeing machine by a microprocessor system

Many claims have been made in the literature as regards the savings that can be made through automation. The principal benefits are undoubtedly the increase in productivity associated with a reduction in the labour required and this is further assisted by the reduction in dyeing cycle times, and fewer additions, rejects and reprocesses. Savings in energy, water, dyes and chemicals are also possible.

It must be emphasized that the results of automation will be disappointing if the control system is simply 'welded on' to an existing operation. Many of the advantages claimed for automation are the result of the discipline which must be imposed before automation is considered.

The most important area for control is the dyeing cycle itself. By means of level sensors and actuated valves, the following functions can be controlled: machine fill, temperature rise, circulation of liquor or material, flow reversal, holding time, cooling time and draining. Other areas where control can be exercised include:

weighing and recording of substrates
selection of correct dye bin in the colour store
monitored weighing of dyes and chemicals
recipe storage and retrieval
controlled dispensing
computer matching, colour correction and colour sorting
inventory control
management information.

A contributory reason for the success of large-batch package dyeing is that a high level of control can be applied, only part of which is the result of automation. The whole matter must be viewed as an overall concept, as outlined in the introduction (see Chapter 1).

The operation of such a system for the control of package dyeing is described briefly below.

The material to be dyed is weighed and the weights of batches waiting to be dyed are recorded by the computer. When a batch is called for dyeing, the computer calculates the recipe required, standard recipes being held in the computer. The recipe is typed out in the dye dispensary and weighing of dyes and chemicals monitored. The dyeing process is controlled by the computer including chemical additions. Management information available includes:

   individual machine and plant status reports
   production reports on a machine and plant basis either in terms of shift or week
   dye and chemical inventory status.

Dispensing tanks are available in the colour dispensary for each dyeing machine and manual panels are available for these and the dyeing machines.

Any system must be reliable and give precise control while giving significant labour savings. It is also beneficial to have control compatibility — interchangeable machine control units — while ancillary systems such as inventory management, costing information and colour physics capabilities, are useful. It is possible to have three levels of control, as described below.

Each machine is controlled by a local panel giving semi-automatic control (time and temperature) with the possibility of manual control in the event of breakdown of the higher control systems. Automatic control of the local panel depends on a mini-computer capable of controlling each machine fully over one dye cycle (time, temperature, valve operation and pumps).

Where there are many machines, each microprocessor is slaved to a system monitor, which registers the state of every machine and presents this information in a simplified form to the supervisor by means of a visual display unit (VDU). On instructions given by the supervisor and information stored in its memory, the system monitor will set up the mini-computer for its next dye cycle. During each dye cycle the system monitor continuously assesses each mini-computer looking for incidents that the mini-computer cannot handle. The system monitor will attempt to assist the mini-computer in correction, but if correction is not possible it will immediately inform the supervisor of the problem and ask for assistance.

Techniques based on colour physics can, with advantage, readily be incorporated into the automated dyehouse. Facilities usually chosen include:

(a)   a match-prediction program, including recipe correction facility and dye evaluation; changes in substrate can also be accommodated

(b)   perpetual inventory programme, which can be interfaced into an existing recorded weighing system

(c)   recipe storage and retrieval, with updating of recipes to allow for changes in substrate or dye quality

(d)   a pass/fail program, used in conjunction with blind-dyeing techniques as a quality control system.

Colour physics technology is now so far advanced that many instrumentally-predicted recipes can be dyed in bulk on a blind-dyeing basis, providing that a high degree of reproducibility is achieved. Further, since the computer can also assess the standardization of dyes, major re-appraisal of purchasing policy is possible.

Future developments in automation of the dyehouse will centre around the use of an automatic press pack and a frame unloader. It will thus be possible to run almost any number of machines with a single operative with packages being fed to the loader from the yarn manufacturing or preparation plant and the unloading device forwarding dyed packages to the next process. Looking further to the future, control by robots must be considered.

A totally automated dyehouse is now feasible, with consequent virtual elimination of labour. The individual stages to which automation must be applied are shown in Table 4.3, together with availability of the necessary control elements.

TABLE 4.3

Individual Stages of Total Automation and Their Current Status

Operation	Already established	Available ITMA 1979	To be developed
Yarn Preparation			
Preparation of package during yarn manufacture	√		
Conveyor to dyehouse with counting and weighing			√
Dyehouse			
Automatic press pack		√	
Automated crane to load frame into dyeing machine	√		
Automation of complete dyeing cycle	√		
Rapid drying with control	√		
Automatic frame unloading		√	
Automated RF dryer for entire drying			√
Dispensary			
Automated dye selection and weighing	√	√	
Recording weighing	√		
Automated solution preparation		√	
Automated dye-liquor preparation		√	
Automated dispensing	√		
Perpetual inventory	√		
Colour Physics/Management Functions			
Cycle logs of machine cycles	√		
Recipe storage and retrieval	√		
Computer match prediction	√		
Instrumental shade pass/fail	√		
Dye delivery testing and recipe up-dating	√		

Table 4.4 compares the productivity from various dyehouses. The future automated package dyehouse is as just described, while in the present automated package dyehouse the dyeing cycles are automated and the dispensary is sited on a mezzanine floor.

TABLE 4.4

Productivity

Process	kg/operative hour
Hank — manual	40
— automated	50
Package — manual	70
— automated (present)	100 to 125
— automated (future)	200 to 250

4.1.8 Dyeing machines for packages

Dyeing machines for packages can be sub-divided into four basic configuration types:

1. *Rectangular dyeing machines,* usually designed for hank dyeing, which have been adapted or further improved to accommodate package frames; these are usually horizontal spindle machines. The outstanding example of this machine type is the Pegg GSH, which is fitted with larger pumps in the package version.
2. *Beam-type dyeing machines,* which have been designed to take horizontal spindle package carriers. These are side-loading machines and examples include the now obsolete Mortensen machine, and the Thies Ecobloc.
3. *Circular dyeing machines,* which are designed to take a number of different types of carrier. These can be used with horizontal spindles or with
4. *Vertical spindle carriers,* the Henriksen GRU range are probably the best known of this type.

There are protagonists for both vertical and horizontal configurations for dyeing. Undoubtedly, satisfactory results with regard to levelness, reproducibility and yarn quality can be obtained from well-designed, properly maintained machines of both types when operated using sound technology. The advantages and disadvantages of the various machine types can be set out briefly as follows:

1. *Rectangular/horizontal spindle type*

   This is usually an economical machine to install and allows hank machines to be converted to dye packages. Although high-temperature versions have been made, they were originally developed as atmospheric machines. Flow rates may be low, so that package density has to be reduced. Only limited press packing is possible and packages may sag on the spindle, giving rise to channelling.

2. *Beam types*

   Usually high-temperature machines, but press packing is limited and sagging may occur on the spindles. Being side loading, less head room is required.

3. *Circular/Horizontal spindle*

   Little advantage is seen with these machines, although it is claimed that a 10% increase in load is possible compared with non-press-packed vertical types. As with all horizontal machines, the payload is much less than when vertical spindles can be used together with press packing. Sagging may occur.

4. *Circular/Vertical spindle*

Press packing is possible with resulting maximum payload, minimum liquor ratio, and savings in resources and dyes. Other features include operation at high-temperature, high and often variable flow rate, and the possibility of direct rapid drying of the packages on frame from the machine. Yarn distortion is minimized, due to press packing. Considerable head room is required, particularly if double-decker cages are used. They are probably the most expensive, but also the most versatile type of machine.

In the author's opinion, this last type of machine, and the technology associated with its operation, which has been outlined earlier, is the best type of package-dyeing machine. This view is obviously shared by machine manufacturers since about 20 of them make such machines. The availability of these is shown in Table 4.5.

TABLE 4.5

Manufacturers of Vertical Spindle Dyeing Machines

Manufacturer	Address
Adaibra	Barcelona, Spain
ATYC	Tarrasa, Barcelona, Spain
Barriquand	Roanne, France
Bellini	Milan, Italy
Bené	Priest mi Plaine, France
Brückner	Erbach, W. Germany
Durand	S/Saone, France
ESPA	Erbach, W. Germany
Gaston County	Stanley, N.C., 28164, U.S.A.
Henriksen	Soeborg, Denmark
Ilma	Schio, Italy
Jaeggli	Winterthur, Switzerland
Jagri	Westfalen, W. Germany
Jasper	Velen/Westf., W. Germany
Krantz	W. Germany
Longclose	Leeds, England
Moliné	Tarrasa, Spain
Obem	Vercelli, Italy
Obermaier	W. Germany
Omli	Vallemosso, Italy
Pegg	Leicester, England
Pozzi	Milan, Italy
Serracant	Sabadell, Barcelona, Spain
Schlumpf	Brunehaut, Hollain, Belgium
Scholl	Switzerland
Termec	Portugal
Then	Schwabisch. Hall-Hessental, W. Germany
Thies	Coesfeld, Westfalen, W. Germany

A machine specification has been proposed and is given in Table 4.6.

TABLE 4.6

Machinery Specification

Spindle diameter (mm)	—	57—72
Spindle centre (mm)	—	215—230
Effective spindle length (m)	—	1.067
Types of frame	—	suitable for range of fibre and package types
Machine sizes (kg)	—	100, 250, 500 and 1000 (approx.)
Liquor ratio	—	to be 10:1 or less
Flow rate (l/kg/min)	—	40—50 (minimum)
Temperature range (°C)	—	to reach 140

It is essential that the spindle diameters, spindle centres and the effective spindle length of package-dyeing frames coincide with the mandrel size on the package-preparation machines, the traverse of the package prepared on such machines allowing for press-packing, as well as with the spindle diameters, etc., of any chamber dryer being used in the system. This means that the total concept of package handling must be considered before deciding on the design details of the dyeing machine itself. For this reason, machines manufactured by Henriksen, with their advanced spindle and pump design, which are known to fit well into the concept of high-bulk acrylic package processing immediately recommend themselves, whereas machines from other manufacturers may require considerable design modification.

When selecting a dyeing machine, methods of pressurizing, pump type, floor space and headroom required, and price are obviously other important factors. Coupling, although sometimes regarded as important, may not be technically advantageous since in a coupled-machine system, it is essential that the flow rate between dye vessels is at least equal to the flow rate within them.

As mentioned earlier, larger diameter spindles favour level dyeing, Pumps may be either of the axial-flow or centrifugal type. A vertical spindle machine in schematic form is illustrated in Figure 4.2.

Developments in package-dyeing machines have included improvements in pump design and spindle geometry, with benefits in circulation. The change from rectangular to circular kiers allows vessels to be more readily pressurized for dyeing above $100°C$. Conventional machines used in current practice should have a flow rate of 30 to 45 litres per kilogram per minute, with a complete circulation of the dye-liquor every 30 seconds. Machines with a flow rate of 50 to 150 l/kg/min, with a complete circulation of the liquor every six seconds at the higher flow rate, are considered to be rapid-dyeing machines. These will allow rates of rise of temperature of 8 to $16°C$ per minute, compared with 2 to $3°C$ per minute on conventional machines. For level dyeing, however, exhaustion rates should not exceed 1 to 3% per liquor circulation.

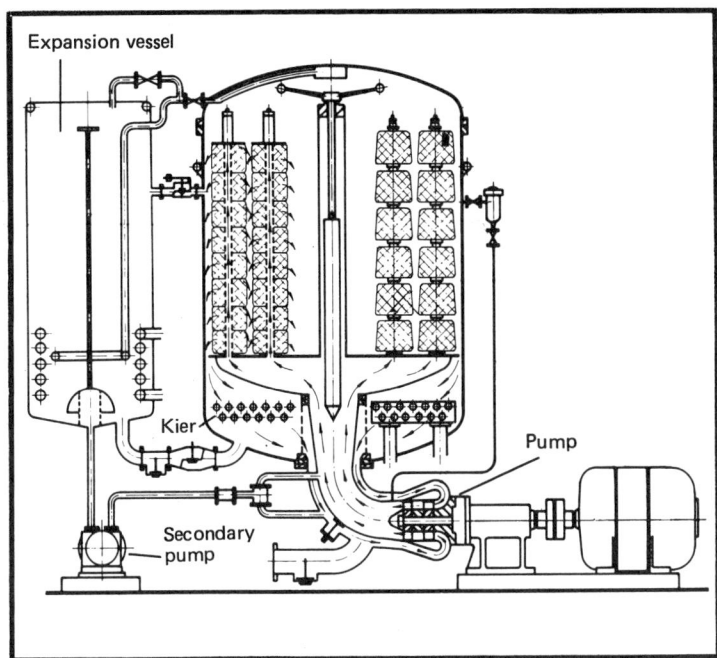

Figure 4.2 — Vertical spindle package-dyeing machine

Developments in rapid-dyeing machines have been extensively reviewed [3]. A recent development has been the ability to run machines partially filled, or with low liquor ratios, as a means of conserving water. Figures 4.3 to 4.6 illustrate the principal types of machines.

Package-dyeing machines are manufactured to operate at temperatures up to the atmospheric boil or at temperatures over 100°C, when pressurized. The former machines are less costly since thinner gauge stainless steel is required and the machines are simpler in design. This type of machine is useful for dyeing fibres which do not require high temperatures, such as wool or cotton, and they are also adequate for bleaching operations. High-temperature machines are more costly since they are most sophisticated in design, require more extensive safety devices, and must be constructed from stainless steel of heavier gauge. These machines are virtually essential for dyeing polyester and are useful for nylon and acrylic fibres, allowing dyeing or, in difficult cases, levelling at 102 to 110°C. To illustrate this point, Henriksen manufacture their GRU package-dyeing range in four basic versions:

the GRU–100°C, which works at atmospheric temperature
the GRU–HTC, which works under static pressure created by compressed air and is available in 110 and 140°C versions,
the GRU–HTB, which works under static pressure created by a pump and operates at up to 140°C.

Figure 4.3 – Pegg GSH horizontal spindle machine

Figure 4.4 – Thies Ecobloc horizontal spindle machine

Figure 4.5 — Henriksen GRU with horizontal spindles

It is usual to install machines of different sizes, the actual size distribution often being dictated by the type of business undertaken. Sewing-thread dyehouses invariably have small machines, with a few larger machines often used to dye blacks and navies and to process white yarn. For machine-knitting yarns and carpet yarns, much larger machines are employed; typical dyelot sizes are 100, 250, 400 and 800 kg. Small machines are expensive, since not only are they more costly in terms of cost per kg of payload but the cost of installation, services and control gear is the same as that for larger machines. Some machine manufacturers vary the payload by changing both the spindle length and the kier size, and hence the number of spindles. Other manufacturers choose to keep the spindle length constant and vary only the kier diameter. This latter method has the advantage that all machines are of a similar height requiring the same headroom. In addition, the concept of utilizing a 'spindle bank' can be operated. This allows detachable spindles to be press-packed individually and loaded into the frames as required.

As mentioned earlier, larger-diameter spindles favour level dyeing, and spindles of various designs are available. These range from perforated spindles with simple circular holes to the more elaborate 'tangential flow' spindles developed by Henriksen. For cones or BI—KO formers, the packages are often dyed on spears with a 'Y' cross-section.

Figure 4.6 — Pegg HTU vertical spindle machine

4.2 HANK PROCESSING

4.2.1 Services

As already indicated, much that has been said about package processing applies equally to the hank form. Modern hank-dyeing machines are amenable to control and, due to their relative simplicity, this is readily achieved. For high-quality results and efficient running, an adequate supply of water, steam and compressed air, delivered by means of satisfactorily installed pipework of the correct material, is required. Modern machines are heated and cooled by closed coils, so that re-use of cooling water is possible and desirable.

Adequate working space is required and, for hank processing, this is likely to be 2000 square feet per tonne of weekly production, if scouring, dyeing and back-winding is to be undertaken. The suitability of a two- or three-tier arrangement in the dyehouse has been mentioned earlier. For the plant as a whole, the traditional 'U'-shaped arrangement will prevent bottlenecks and ensure efficient work flow.

The capacity for scouring, dyeing, drying and back-winding should be in balance with due regard to the variety of yarns processed and the overall production mix.

4.2.2 Dyeing machines

For many centuries, until the early decades of the twentieth century, hank dyeing was carried out in primitive equipment in which the yarn hanks were suspended on wooden poles in a rectangular wooden vat. The sticks were moved from end to end of the vat to give some degree of agitation and at the same time the hanks were turned manually to prevent the formation of undyed areas if the yarn remained in contact with the sticks. The gradual mechanization of this system and the replacement of wood by metal, and ultimately by stainless steel, resulted in the development of the 'Hussong' machine. This type of machine has been made by most manufacturers and is still widely used, especially in the carpet industry. Such a machine is illustrated diagramatically in Figure 4.7.

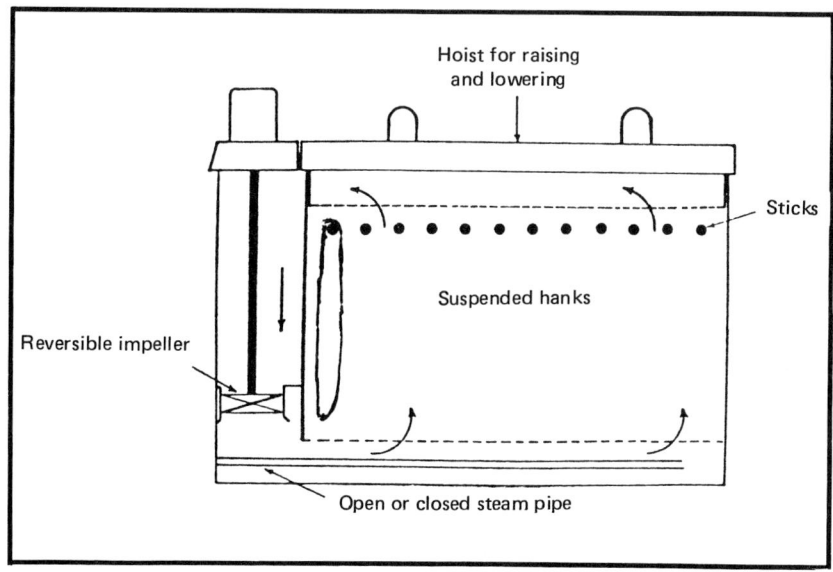

Figure 4.7 — Hussong hank-dyeing machine

Heating is by open- or closed-coil steam pipes, which are situated below a perforated false bottom. The dye-liquor is circulated over a weir and through the yarn by means of a reversible impeller. In modern machines, the yarn is suspended from V-shaped sticks with perforations to prevent stick marking. Even so, with some qualities, the yarn is turned on the sticks manually half-way through the dyeing process. When the temperature in the bath reaches about 70°C, the yarn is removed, stick by stick, and turned so that the section previously over the stick lies in a new position. A further precaution to ensure level dyeing in machines with low flow is to replace the sticks in a different position in the frame following turning.

Most developments and variations in the design of hank-dyeing machines have probably been intended to overcome the problems of stick marking and the general poor flow characteristics of the machine. These developments have, until fairly recently, followed two distinct lines. The first was based on improvements to the rectangular-type machine, of which the Hussong was the forerunner. The second trend in development was to find a method to rotate the yarn on the sticks throughout the process. For historical reasons, this latter method will be discussed first.

4.2.3 Rotating-stick machines

In the Gerber-type of machine, which is illustrated in Figure 4.8, the hanks are suspended from rods made of porcelain or some similar smooth-surface material.

Figure 4.8 – Rotating horizontal-arm hank-dyeing machine

These horizontal arms rotate over the becks in which the yarn is suspended and a reciprocating vertical motion can also be given. The rollers also reverse automatically. This type of machine has been widely used to dye cotton and rayon yarns.

In the Klauder—Weldon machine, the hanks are held on wooden rods in a carrier consisting of two larger and two smaller concentric wheels. The hanks are moved through the dye-liquor by rotating the whole wheel assembly. By means of projections on the outer sticks and fixed strikers fitted to the side of the bath, the hanks are caused to revolve. As mentioned earlier, this machine was also useful for wet-setting processes. The principle of the machine is shown in Figure 4.9 and illustrated in Figure 4.10.

Both of the machines discussed in this section are virtually obsolete, but both of them, in their day, made possible useful advances in hank-dyeing methods and for this reason are included here.

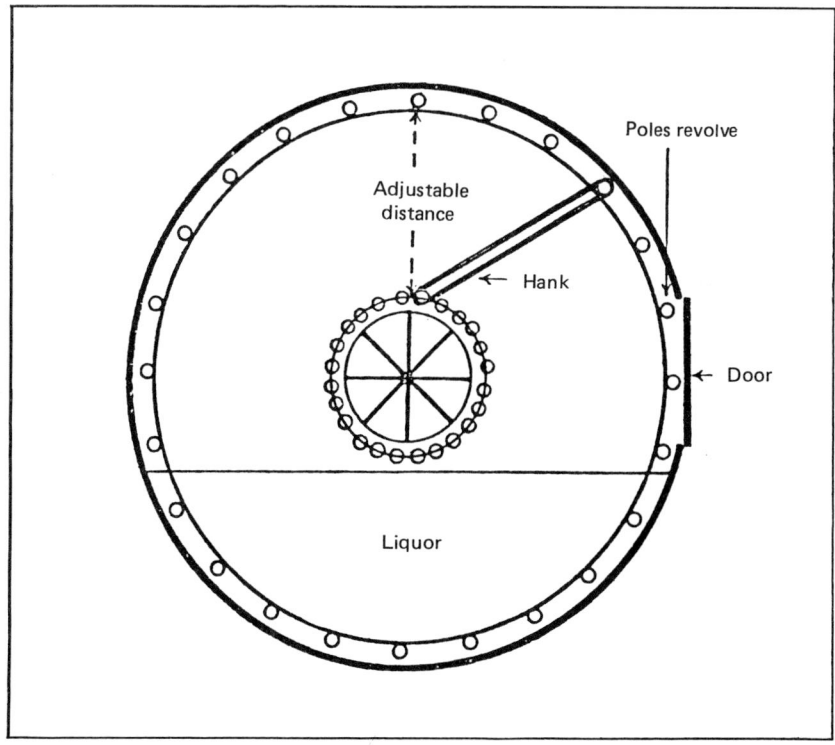

Figure 4.9 — Principle of the Klauder—Weldon machine

Figure 4.10 — The Klauder-Weldon machine

4.2.4 Developments in rectangular machines

Early improvements in the Hussong type of machine centred around the follow-ing modifications:

- the use of closed steam coils
- large-diameter double-scroll propellers running at slow speeds to reduce turbulence
- perforated sticks
- central impeller compartments to reduce distance of flow
- machine coupling, especially in the carpet industry, to enable larger batches to be dyed.

The Pegg Pulsator machine is a much modified version of the Hussong, is more compact and, it is claimed, gives an improved quality yarn. The principle of the machine is illustrated in Figure 4.11.

As can be seen, there is no false bottom, the steam pipe is sited in the small end section and the impeller shaft is horizontal. The yarn is suspended from poles in the usual manner, but is relatively tightly packed so that stainless steel

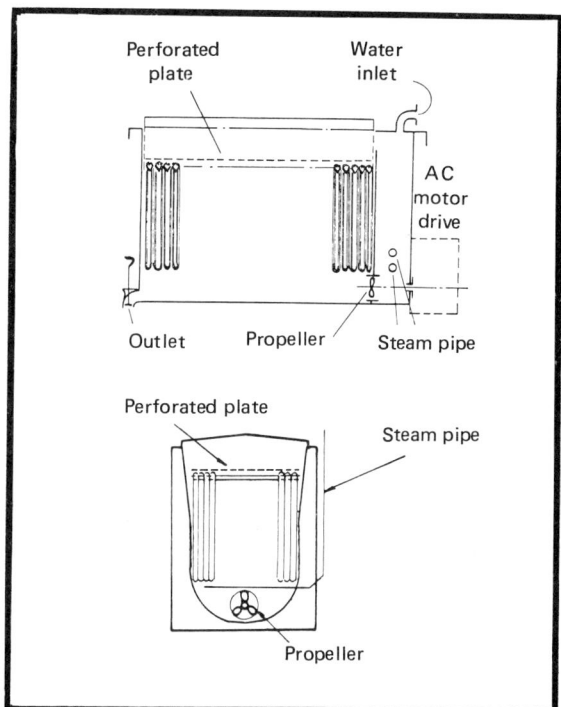

Figure 4.11 — Principle of the Pegg Pulsator machine

end plates are required to keep the mass together. The unique feature of this machine, as its name implies, is the pulsator mechanism. The flow of liquor is automatically interrupted for 5 to 10 seconds every 2½ minutes, thereby giving a pulsing movement which raises the hanks off the sticks and prevents stick-marking. The direction of flow is upwards through the impeller compartment and down through the hanks. Downward flow can also be used, if required. Due to its compact nature, liquor ratios of 10:1 can be obtained as opposed to the 20:1 normally encountered in hank machines. Machines ranging from 5 to 600-kg capacity are available and machine coupling is possible.

The pulsator principle and the possibility of flow reversal encouraged development of automatic controls for hank-dyeing machines. Pulsators can also be fitted with a bottom set of sticks, thereby converting them to two-stick machines.

In one-stick machines of the Hussong type, the direction of flow is mainly up through the hanks which causes the yarn to form a dense pack which impedes liquor flow. This causes unlevel dyeing, particularly if dyes of higher wet fastness (with inferior levelling characteristics) must be used. The use of a second stick at the bottom of the hanks prevents the mass being lifted by the flow and allows a greater rate of flow to be used without severe tangling. Two-stick machines, capable of operating at temperatures above 100°C, have also been developed.

Two-stick machines take longer to load and unload than the conventional one-stick machine. Since both types of machine are labour-intensive, each machine is usually purchased with a number of frames to ease bottlenecks. On two-stick machines, the distance between sticks must be adjusted according to the hank length, so that the yarn is not stretched tight during dyeing. If this occurs, severe stick marking at both the top and bottom of the hanks will occur. It is customary to leave about 4 cm free space between the bottom stick and the hank. This adjustment is much more critical when high-bulk yarns are being processed, since allowance must be made for the shrinkage which will occur in the hank as bulk is developed.

Well-known machines of this type include:

— the ILMA two-stick machine
— F.T.M. 'Plusflo' machine
— Farrar double-stick machine
— Platt-Longclose TC two-stick machine

4.2.5 The Pegg GSH hank-dyeing machine

This is a double-stick machine which was designed especially for dyeing high-bulk acrylic and most types of hand-knitting yarn. The principle of the machine is shown in Figure 4.12.

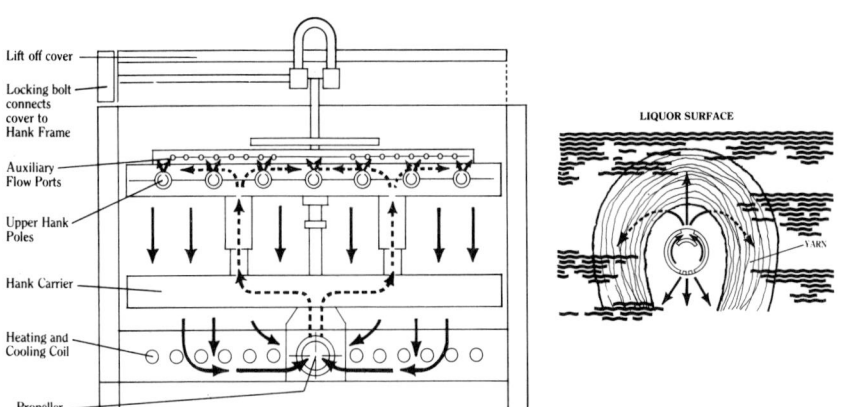

Figure 4.12 — The Pegg GSH machine for hanks

A horizontal propeller shaft circulates liquor in one direction only, up a narrow central compartment, which forms part of the frame, over and through the tops of the hanks and down through the hanks, returning to the propeller. The unique feature of this machine is that a regulated proportion of the dye-liquor is directed, by adjustable slots, from the central compartment through the top hank poles. The hanks are thus lifted slightly off the poles to prevent stick marking. This machine gives a gentle, but uniform, liquor flow through the yarn pack, with minimum yarn entanglement, eliminates temperature differences through the pack and prevents glazing and flattening of the yarn. The hank sticks are readily adjustable by means of a central wheel on top of the frame allowing for a range of hank reel lengths as well as giving the same liquor ratio for different hank lengths.

In some versions of the machine, the bottom sticks have been omitted without detriment to the yarn quality. Pressurized versions of the machine, operating at temperatures of 105 or 110°C are available and these can be used to advantage to level faulty dyeings or in dyehouses situated at high altitudes.

As has been discussed earlier, this machine, with a suitable frame and a slightly higher capacity pump, can be used to dye packages, particularly those of high-bulk acrylic yarn.

4.2.6 Circular, multi-purpose machines

More recently, as a further development in machinery, several machine manufacturers have developed cages for dyeing hanks, to fit into circular machines originally intended for dyeing yarn in other forms. This type of machine enables the dyehouse to be versatile in that loose fibre, and yarn in various forms, including hank, can be dyed in one machine, provided that the necessary type of carrier is available. These machines are readily available for high-temperature dyeing; for dyeing hank, the two-stick principle is used, as illustrated in Figure 4.13.

Figure 4.13 — Circular hank frame

Two-way flow is normally employed, but a disadvantage of this type of machine is the higher capital cost compared to conventional dyeing machines for hank. The hank sticks are situated in concentric circles round the frame and, since each consecutive circle accomodates a different number of hanks, loading must be carried out with care. The distance between sticks is adjustable to allow for different hank lengths and, in general, the earlier comments regarding two-stick machines apply here.

Circular cages are not easy to load and the process is labour-intensive. Because of this, plus the high capital cost of the machine together with the lower loads of hank in a given machine compared to those possible with other materials, this is a costly method of hank processing. Loadings for various types of material are compared in Table 4.7.

Hanks can also be dyed in annular-type, loose-stock baskets; this method has been used for muffs of continuous filament yarn. High-twist carpet yarn for the production of 'kinky' carpets is also processed in this way since it allows for the relaxation of the yarn and full development of the twist.

TABLE 4.7

Comparative Machine Loads on Circular Machines

Form of Material	Relative Machine Capacity
Hank	
Wool	100
High-bulk acrylic	75
Cotton	170
Basket Method	
Loose stock	190
Tops	225
Muffs	125
Packages	
Wool and cotton	220
Continuous filament	200
Acrylic	200

4.2.7 Machine manufacturers

Several machine manufacturers offer hank-dyeing equipment. These are listed in Table 4.8. Those companies which make multi-purpose machines are also indicated.

With conventional dyeing machines for hank, a two-tier layout in the dye-house would be satisfactory, since the pumps are usually sited alongside the machine. With the circular type, a three-tier layout would be required to house the pumps and services below the machine. This is a further point to take into account in any costing on machine installation.

TABLE 4.8

Manufacturers of Hank-dyeing Machines

Manufacturer	Multi-purpose machines	Address
Adaibra	√	Barcelona, Spain
ATYC		Tarassa, Spain
Bellini		Milan, Italy
Henriksen	√	Soeborg, Denmark
ILMA	√	Schio, Italy
Jagri	√	Westfalen, W. Germany
Longclose	√	Leeds, England
Mezzera		Milan, Italy
Moliné		Tarassa, Spain
Obermaier	√	Neustadt, W. Germany
Pegg	√	Leicester, England
Then	√	Schwabisch Hall-Hessental, W. Germany

4.2.8 Comments on machine loading

Reference has already been made to the importance of loading machines correctly, since this can have considerable influence on yarn quality. In general, rectangular single-stick machines have a relatively poor flow rate which can lead to 'dead spots' in the corners of the vessel. With rectangular machines, it is important that equal numbers of hanks are placed on each stick to avoid channelling and thus unlevel dyeing. Similarly, over-loading will lead to unlevel dyeing, while under-loading may cause the same problem due to channelling as well as the added problem of yarn tangling. The maximum amount of yarn to be loaded into a machine of a given size also depends on yarn and fibre type. This is indicated in Table 4.9 for Pegg GSH machines.

TABLE 4.9

Comparative Pegg GSH Loadings

Yarn Type	Relative Loading
High bulk acrylic hosiery yarn	100
Wool and regular acrylic hosiery yarn	130
Carpet yarn	150

With two-stick machines, the same comments apply with the additional precaution that room must be left below the bottom stick to allow for the hanks to rise when the flow is reversed. This is normally about 4 cm. In this respect, allowance must be made for the shrinkage which occurs during processing of high-bulk yarn.

On circular machines, as already mentioned, each consecutive stick in the concentric circles will require to be loaded with a different number of hanks. Guidance will be given by the machine manufacturer, but each dyehouse will require to reach the correct loadings for the individual yarns being processed. The distance between sticks is an important factor with circular machines.

With machines of all types, careful loading and 'dressing' of hanks on to the sticks will greatly assist in obtaining level results by the elimination of twists, snarls and so forth. This will also influence waste generation, both in dyeing and at subsequent hank-to-cone winding.

4.2.9 Machine type and yarn quality

The levelness of the dyed yarn is determined by liquor flow and choice of process, including dye selection. Thus the quality of yarn in this respect will depend on the efficiency of the machine used. A further measure of yarn quality is the bulk of the yarn produced, together with its windability and the waste generated. Short dyeing cycles, often as a result of blind-dyeing techniques, preserve the physical properties of the yarn. Machines which give least yarn entanglement are also beneficial.

In practice, it has been found that the Pegg GSH machine gives dyed yarn of high quality. Not only are level dyeings produced but, in addition, least waste is generated during winding, little entanglement occurs and maximum bulking effects are obtained, particularly with high-bulk acrylic yarns. While dyelots of good levelness are obtained from circular two-stick machines, the yarn is less bulky, waste figures are high and there is more entanglement. This may be the result of the higher speed, two-way flow. This effect has been confirmed for both hosiery and carpet yarns.

REFERENCES

1. Little, *Water Supplies and the Treatment and Disposal of Effluents,* Textile Institute Monograph Number 2 (1975).
2. Bialik, Park and Walker, *Rev. Prog. Coloration,* **10** (1979) 55.
3. Siegrist, ibid., **8** (1977) 24.

CHAPTER 5

Drying

5.1 PACKAGES

Following dyeing, it is necessary to remove the water from the dyed material
before subsequent processing. Various methods are available for packages, and
these vary in their cost, suitability and efficiency. The main methods will now be
considered in turn.

5.1.1 Hydro-extraction by centrifuge

This is undoubtedly the cheapest available method of removing water from packages since there are no heating costs. In principle, the packages are placed in a
basket, which rotates at a sufficiently high speed to remove a large proportion of
the water by centrifugal force. Conventional, slow-speed extractors rotate at
about 375 r.p.m. and take a relatively long time (up to 45 min) to reduce the
moisture content to 25 to 35% depending on the fibre. The yarn so treated
invariably requires to be dried further in a thermal type dryer.

   High-speed extractors rotate at 1450 r.p.m. and will reduce the moisture
content of synthetic yarns to between 4 and 8% in about 10 minutes. After the
normal delay time the yarn is then in an ideal condition for winding without
further drying. Unfortunately, rigid centres can be destroyed or seriously
distorted under the high G-force developed, so that high-speed extractors are
best suited to packages prepared on non-woven fabric centres.

   Conventional hydro-extractors are intensive in labour since packages
require to be loaded and unloaded. With high-speed versions, the packages can
be loaded into bags directly from the dyeing frame and these bags are lifted by
means of a small hoist in and out of the centrifuge with considerable labour
savings. An interesting development of the centrifuge is that by Frauchiger in
which packages are handled individually, but this requires one person to attend
to the machine continuously.

5.1.2 Thermal chambers

Following low-speed hydro-extraction or even high-speed extraction of natural
fibres, final drying is necessary. This is usually carried out in a thermal drying
chamber, in which the packages are loaded on perforated spindles or some
similar arrangement and hot air is blown through. Typical drying times are

45–60 minutes at 100 to 110°C to reduce the moisture content from 25 to 4%.

The cost of the drying process is significantly increased using this method since not only are substantial quantities of energy required, but the process is also labour intensive.

5.1.3 Rapid drying

The wet yarn on the drying frame can be lifted directly into a rapid dryer such as that illustrated in Figure 5.1.

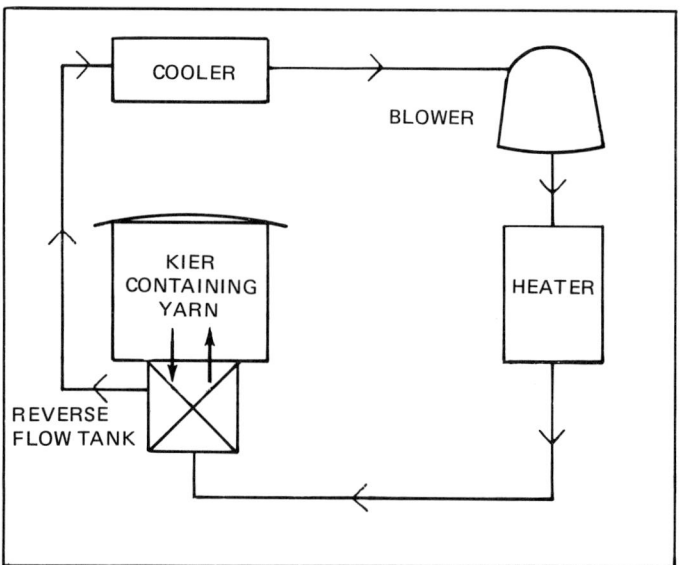

Figure 5.1. — Rapid dryer

This method is economical in labour but expensive in energy. A typical drying sequence is as follows:

Extraction of excess water with high-velocity cold air, out/in circulation	10 minutes
Drying — in/out circulation of hot air at 100°C	60 minutes
Uniform redistribution of remaining moisture, out/in circulation	10 minutes

Rapid drying can only be really successful with press-packed material since air tends to find the easiest route through the material. Drying times for various fibres, claimed by one maker of rapid-drying machines, are given in Table 5.1.

TABLE 5.1

Rapid Drying Times

	Time for 500-kg load (min)
Acrylic	40
Cotton	60
Wool	50

5.1.4 Radio-frequency drying

One of the most interesting recent developments in the area of drying has been the use of radio-frequency (RF) techniques. This can be used as a final drying technique, in place of, for example, chamber drying, following hydro-extraction in the normal way. Alternatively, in a machine designed by Dawson International and built by Strayfield, the whole drying operation can be carried out in one machine, in this case by applying suction to the individual packages before they enter the RF zone. The RF technique offers large savings in energy and has no adverse effects on fibres such as wool, since over-drying cannot occur. Production rates compare very favourably with the figures quoted above for rapid drying, even though the operation can be labour intensive. However, this can be reduced by allying the final RF process with, for example, the well-known Frauchiger hydro-extractor, so that one operative services both machines.

5.1.5 Cost and productivity

It has been mentioned earlier that drying processes vary considerably in cost. An indication of this and the productivity which can be obtained from the various methods is given in Table 5.2.

TABLE 5.2

Drying Cost and Productivity

	Cost* (p/kg)	*Production* (kg/hour)
Hydro-extract only	1.0	250
Hydro + package cabinet	7.0	260
Rapid dryer	10.0	400
RF	5.0	250

*(includes wages, electricity, steam, depreciation and other overheads)

5.2 HANKS

Following dyeing, the hanks are removed from the frames and often tied into
bunches by looping one hank through several others. Drying is then necessary
before further processing, the bulk of the water being removed by mechanical
means.

5.2.1 Mechanical water removal

Undoubtedly, the cheapest and most efficient mechanical way of removing
water is by centrifuging. The hanks are placed in a basket which is rotated at
sufficient speed to remove a high proportion of the water. Depending on
whether high- or low-speed machines are used and also on fibre type — principally whether synthetic or natural fibre yarn is being processed — hydro-
extraction by centrifuge will reduce the moisture content to values from 4 to
35%.
    An alternative method of removing water from hanks is by squeezing, using a
pair of rollers similar to those situated between the bowls of a continuous
scouring machine. Indeed, as previously mentioned, this procedure can be used
to apply chemicals, such as the soft finish to acrylic yarns, after dyeing. Even
with several tonnes pressure on the rollers, the residual moisture content can still
be as high as 60%.

5.2.2 Thermal chambers

Yarns manufactured from natural fibres require to be dried further by hot air to
reduce the moisture content to an acceptable level. An early method of doing
this was to use a drying room or 'stove'. This room would be say 60 feet long by
20 feet wide and 6 to 8 feet high so that an average-sized man could walk in to
load poles with yarn. Two sets of poles were provided, one being situated above
the other, and supported from wooden beams which ran the length of the room
at two levels. The room would probably be designed to hold a day's production,
since drying took several hours. Heat was supplied by a bank of steam pipes
situated at one end of the room and the hot air was circulated by fans situated
at the other end. Ventilation for the removal of moisture was also provided.
    This method was labour intensive, since it took several hours to fill the room.
When this was accomplished, the doors were shut, the steam and fans turned on.
After several hours, the yarn would be dry and the process was carried out in
reverse to empty the room. One advantage of this method was that over-drying
was not likely. A problem could arise if the water content of the
extracted hanks varied. This could cause hanks to extend to different lengths
while hanging, thus causing slight changes in count, and could result in the
production of stripey material, particularly carpets.
    Modern drying techniques depend on the hanks being loaded on to sticks
similar to those used in dyeing. These sticks are placed on two endless belts

which in turn take the hanks through a heated chamber. One man feeds the machine while another strips the poles at the exit end. Such a machine is shown in Figure 5.2.

Figure 5.2 — Thermal hank dryer

In addition to drying, this process also helps to straighten the yarn and leave it in an ideal condition for subsequent back-winding. Yarns which do not really require drying after centrifuging, such as acrylics, may be fed through this machine with only cold air circulating, to bring about the hank straightening.

An alternative to this type of machine is a thermal drier based on the Fleissner suction drum principle. In this case, hanks are processed individually on a belt feed and no straightening effect is obtained.

Recent developments in drying have included machines capable of handling jumbo hanks. Minnetti has been in the forefront of this development and manufactures dryers, particularly for the carpet industry, in which squeezing to remove the bulk of the moisture is an integral part of the operation. Two men can operate a drying range for jumbo hanks, including loading and unloading the dryer, and packing. This type of machine is claimed to have a production rate of 2800 kg per hour.

5.2.3 Radio-frequency drying

Following hydro-extraction, radio-frequency drying techniques can be used as a final drying treatment. Conveyor-type machines are used in which individual hanks are fed on to an endless belt which transports the yarn through the RF field. This is again a two-man operation and is thus labour intensive. However, savings in energy and preservation of yarn quality are claimed, especially since over-drying cannot occur.

CHAPTER 6

Dye selection and dyeing processes

6.1 GENERAL PHILOSOPHY OF DYE SELECTION

It is becoming increasingly recognized that the basic philosophy of dye selection should be to obtain the maximum gamut of shades using the minimum number of dyes. This is not only because it is possible to meet all criteria using relatively few dyes, and technical staff can remember the properties of these, but also because by using the minimum number of dyes substantial savings in stock holding can be achieved, with the associated benefit in cash flow, plus the price advantage of bulk buying. It is thus possible to have only 10—15 dyes on average per substrate and even a smaller number in some cases. Although price of the product, in terms of £ per kilo is important, cost-effectiveness is much more relevant. Products which give a high degree of reproducibility with shortened cycle times are desirable.

The technical factors on which dyes are selected include the following:

Shade and metamerism, colour consistency under various illuminants
Levelling properties as dictated by available machinery
Fastness — over the maximum number of end-uses
Compatibility with other dyes and auxiliaries
Reproducibility
Temperature stability
pH stability
Cost/colour value
Penetration
Minimum staining of other fibres
Coverage of irregularities in the substrate
Homogeneity
Build up in dark shades
Dusting
Health hazards
Particle size
Solubility ⎫
Physical form ⎬ can be of special relevance
Dispersion stability ⎭ in package dyeing

When selecting dyes to produce a particular shade, there are two basic methods of approach. In the first method, a dye is chosen which is close to the shade required and small amounts of shading colour are added to produce the desired shade. This method gives a high degree of reproducibility and the best chance of level results, particularly if the concept of using internal primaries and colour mapping is employed. This technique has been well documented [1]. This method of approach is possible with dye classes such as 1:2 metal-complex dyes, direct, vat and a few other types where homogeneous dyes exist to cover the complete colour gamut.

The alternative approach is to base the majority of shades on a ternary combination of bright primary dyes and to supplement this by a small range of dyes with which they are compatible to give a wider gamut of shades, particularly with reference to brightness and depth. This triangulation approach is shown in Figure 6.1.

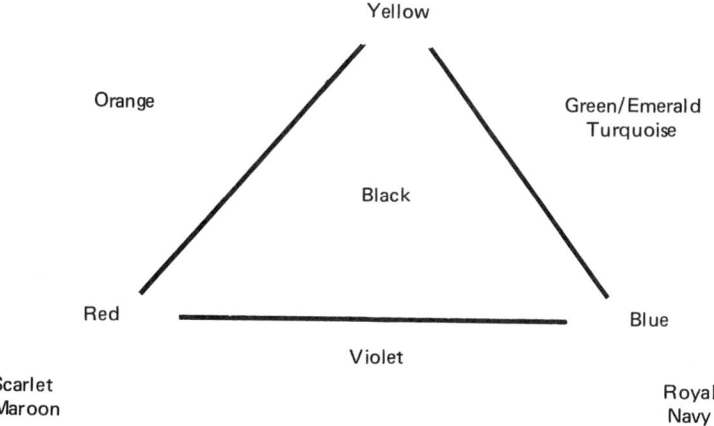

Figure 6.1 – Selection of dyes by triangulation

Approximately 12 dyes are required and this method is used when homogeneous dyes are not available over the entire colour gamut. Examples of dye classes where this occurs are equalizing acid dyes, basic dyes, disperse dyes and reactive dyes.

As has been mentioned earlier, dyes for package dyeing require to be chosen with regard to particle size, dispersion stability and solubility due to the filtration effect that can be exerted by the packages of yarn. Similar comments apply to the use of auxiliaries and chemicals. The selection of retarders is discussed in some detail later, but dispersing agents should also be chosen with care. Systems which depend on the formation of complexes between agent and dyes require careful handling. Foam in the dyebath can reduce the efficiency of pumps and reduce the flow rate, thereby increasing the possibility of unlevel results, so that anti-foaming agents are usually required in the dyebath.

In commercial terms, moisture content, price-*vs*-strength and continuity in both quantity and quality (standardization) are important. It is equally important to use correct dispensing and application techniques. The ultimate aim is to achieve a high degree of reproducibility with no reprocessing being necessary either on shade, fastness or levelness grounds.

In the author's opinion, it is only after selection has been carried out on the basis of the above screening tests, that computer match prediction should be utilized. In this case, the computer is only at liberty to select dyes from a well-defined group of otherwise technically suitable products. As mentioned earlier, computer matching with its facilities for dye evaluation may enable purchasing policies to be changed with consequent financial savings. In addition, when alternative dye classes or members of a dye class are available for matching a given shade, the most economical method can be selected within the limit of technical adequacy.

A high degree of reproducibility must also be achieved, both between laboratory and bulk and between bulk batches. This is assisted by giving attention to many of the factors enumerated earlier, such as accurate weighing, standard methods and so on. Determination of the dyeing characteristics of the substrate, so that dyeing conditions can be defined, is also necessary; application techniques based on calculation methods should be used where possible. The use of easily dispensable products, such as liquid dyes, should be considered whenever available.

With some fibres, such as acrylic, wool and nylon, it is often possible to select a short range of dyes from a given dye class which will be satisfactory for a number of end uses. With disperse dyes for polyester, on the other hand, it may be necessary to have a different range of dyes for each end use.

In general terms, for package dyeing, dyes of intrinsically high fastness properties are employed, not purely on the grounds of the fastness of the dyeing but because these dyes generally give a high level of reproducibility.

The general philosophy of dye selection for hank dyeing, and the overall properties of the dyes required, do not differ significantly from those discussed above for package dyeing. In many cases, hank-dyed and package-dyed yarns are used for the same purposes and, therefore, must possess similar properties.

As has been stated previously, the flow rate and circulation properties of hank machines are relatively poor. Indeed, many of the older versions of the machine are totally unsuitable for applying certain classes of dye to certain fibre types, if level results are to be obtained. Because of this restriction, the hank-dyeing process requires to be modified in two ways:

1. Dyes with better levelling properties should be used whenever possible and when the end use allows, even at the loss of a degree of fastness and reproducibility.
2. The application process should be adjusted where possible, e.g. by the use of lower rates of temperature rise.

6.1.1 Fastness requirements

Although it is not intended to discuss the fastness requirements of dyed yarns in detail, comments are made in the text when some outstanding fastness property is required. Requirements vary according to end use, but the usual fastness properties which must be met are as follows:

Light
Washing
Perspiration
Dry cleaning
Wet and dry rubbing
Water
Gas fume fading
Sublimation
Chlorinated water
Cross-dyeing

For carpets, the principal fastness requirements are:

Light
Sea water
Water
Shampooing.

6.2 ACRYLIC YARNS IN PACKAGE FORM

6.2.1 Disperse dyes

Disperse dyes can be used to dye acrylic fibres, since they allow rapid dyeing, with good levelling, but they are not used above about 0.5% depth because they exhibit poor build-up properties and poor wet fastness. In addition, soft finishes, applied to most acrylic fibres after dyeing to enhance the handle are applied in a fresh bath. This can off-set any advantage obtained by this simple process.
    The packages are entered and the dyebath is prepared at 50°C with:

1.0% Acetic acid (80%) to adjust the pH of the bath to 5
1.0% of a Dispersing agent (such as Sunaptol LT) (Alliance)
0.5% of Ethylene diamine tetra acetic acid — EDTA — (sequestering agent)
and the Dye.

    The temperature of the dyebath is raised rapidly to the boil, and dyeing continued at the boil for 30 minutes. Additions can be made at 95°C. When on shade, the bath is cooled to 60°C at 1.5°C per minute and dropped.
    A soft finish is applied in a fresh bath at 55°C for 15 minutes.
    A typical ternary combination of disperse dyes for acrylic yarn is:

C.I. Disperse Yellow 3
C.I. Disperse Red 59
C.I. Disperse Blue 3.

With the availability of dispensing facilities, the chemicals are prepared and sent to the dyebath as the first addition and the dye as a second addition. The disperse dyes are dispensed by adding the dry powder slowly to about 30 times their own weight of water at 50–60°C in the mixing tank, with the stirrer on.

6.2.2 Basic (cationic) dyes

The majority of shades on acrylic fibres are obtained with basic dyes since they give highly reproducible dyeing of excellent fastness. They generally give a high colour value at relatively low cost. The production of level dyeings may be a problem, but this can be overcome using retarders with dyes of similar compatibility. Basic dyes are categorized for compatibility on a 1 to 5 scale of CV (or K) values, the lower the number the more rapid the strike. For yarn package dyeing, CV3 dyes are generally used, since a large gamut of shades can be obtained from a limited range of dyes. CV1 dyes may be used for low affinity fibres and the production of dark shades. These latter dyes are also used on fibres such as latent crimp (bicomponent) Courtelle, since they give best solidity between the components.

Retarders may be either cationic or anionic in nature, with the former type being almost exclusively used on 100% acrylic materials.

Anionic retarders complex with the cationic dye, which is released slowly from the complex as dyeing proceeds. They are the more expensive type, but do not lead to blocking problems, while the selection of dyes according to CV value is unimportant. Anionic retarders tend to be dye-specific and a nonionic dispersing agent is normally required in the dyebath to keep the dye – retarder complex in solution.

With cationic retarders, in the early stages the smaller-molecular-weight retarder is absorbed on to the available dye sites in the fibre and then released as dyeing proceeds, thus allowing dye to reach the dye sites. The CV factor of the retarder should be preferably only slightly lower than that of the dyes used which in turn should have similar CV values. This type of retarder system is said to be less expensive in chemical cost and is readily adjustable to allow for the different dyeing properties of acrylic yarns, but dyes must be selected according to CV value. The amount of cationic retarder required depends, in essence, on such fibre factors as saturation (S_f) and rate of dyeing (V). The percentage retarder required to give an exhausted dyebath in a given time at an appropriate dyeing temperature is calculated from data supplied by the dyemaker. By this means, acrylic fibres of widely differing dyeing characteristics can be dyed satisfactorily.

Cationic retarders may be temporary or permanent in their effect, depending on whether the cationic activity is lost by hydrolysis. Recent work has shown that, with some retarders, the retarding effect remains even if the retarder is boiled for an hour in the blank dyebath before the dyeing cycle is carried out. This may mean that the difference in effect between retarders is due to differences in molecular weight or shape, which defines their ease of removal from the fibre and their replacement by dye.

In dyeing, realistic dyeing times should be achieved and exhaustion should be obtained in a maximum time of 90—120 minutes. Long dyeing times, as a result of excess retarder, may alter the dyeing characteristics of the fibre significantly, and dye hydrolysis may also occur.

To obtain optimum results, as far as levelness is concerned, it is necessary to: —

(a)   select dyes of similar CV values
(b)   know the dyeability parameters of the fibre being dyed — usually the saturation value
      (S_f) and the rate of dyeing (V);
(c)   calculate, from the values obtained for (b), and from the properties of the dyes being
      used, the amount of retarder required.

6.2.3 Determination of dyeing parameters of fibre

The saturation value of unknown polyacrylonitrile fibres can be found in the laboratory in the following manner:

The fibre under investigation is dyed in four separate baths containing 1% acetic acid (60%) in a liquor ratio of 40:1 with 4, 5, 7 and 9% Astrazone Blue FRR (Bayer). A control dyeing is made at the same time with 7% Astrazone Blue FRR on Dralon or another acrylic fibre with a saturation value of 2.1. After dyeing for 3—4 hours at the boil, dyebath exhaustion is determined by carrying out an exhaustion dyeing on the same material. The saturation value of the unknown fibre is found by comparing the four exhaustion dyeings with that of the control dye and selecting the one which most closely resembles that of the control, as follows:

4% Astrazone Blue FRR = S_f 1.2
5% Astrazone Blue FRR = S_f 1.5
7% Astrazone Blue FRR = S_f 2.1
9% Astrazone Blue FRR = S_f 2.7

Intermediate values can be estimated.

The dyeing rate of acrylic fibres, like the saturation value, is easily determined in the laboratory:

Equal parts by weight of the fibre to be tested and of a fibre with a known dyeing rate are dyed in a single bath containing 2% Astrazone Blue FRR and 1.5% acetic acid (60%) until the bath is exhausted. Equal depth of shade on both fibres indicates equal dyeing rates. If the unknown fibre is paler or deeper than the control, its dyeing rate is correspondingly lower or higher. If the strength difference is more than 20%, the test should be repeated with another control fibre with a lower or higher dyeing rate.

6.2.4 Calculation of quantity of retarder required

The basic premise is that, for a given fibre, there are a total number of dye sites which must be occupied by dye plus retarder molecules to give level dyeing. A fibre with a given S_f and V value will thus have a total concentration value. Such values are given in Table 6.1.

TABLE 6.1

Total Concentration Values

Fibre Type		Dyes				
Dyeing Rate	Saturation value of the fibre			CV value		
V	S_f	1	2	3	4	5
1.0—1.5	1.0	1.25	1.12	0.83	0.64	0.41
	1.2	1.47	1.31	0.98	0.75	0.52
	1.4	1.66	1.47	1.14	0.86	0.60
	2.2	2.50	2.18	1.74	1.36	0.98
1.6—2.0	1.2	1.55	1.39	1.08	0.84	0.60
	1.4	1.75	1.57	1.22	0.96	0.67
	1.8	2.16	1.92	1.53	1.21	0.89
	2.1	2.41	2.20	1.71	1.41	1.05
	2.2	2.63	2.33	1.87	1.50	1.12
	2.8	3.20	2.82	2.29	1.84	1.38
2.1—3.5	1.2	1.55	1.51	1.21	0.97	0.73
	1.4	1.81	1.71	1.37	1.11	0.84
	1.8	2.34	2.08	1.69	1.38	1.05
	2.2	2.73	2.43	1.98	1.60	1.23
	2.8	3.40	3.01	2.48	2.03	1.57
3.6—5.0	1.2	1.55	1.51	1.32	1.21	1.00
	1.4	1.81	1.76	1.57	1.38	1.10
	1.8	2.34	2.26	1.93	1.61	1.30
	2.2	2.85	2.70	2.25	1.88	1.50
	2.8	3.62	3.24	2.72	2.25	1.80
Over 5.0	2.2	2.85	2.78	2.55	2.40	2.04
	2.8	3.62	3.55	3.25	2.80	2.34

The steps required for the calculation of the amount of a cationic retarder such as Astrazone Retarder PAN (Bayer) or Matexil LC—RA (ICI) are as follows:

(a) Using the S_f and V values obtained for the fibre being dyed, read off from Table 6.1 the total concentration value. Where a mixture of dyes is being used the lower CV value should be taken. A list of typical S_f and V values are given in Table 6.2.

(b) Calculate the dye concentration value by multiplying the percentage of each dye by its f factor. A list of basic dyes which are suitable, and which will be dealt with more fully later, is given in Table 6.3. together with their CV and f values.

(c) Subtract dye concentration value (b) from total concentration value (a) to give the percentage retarder required.

TABLE 6.2

Dyeing Parameters of Acrylic Fibres

	V	S_f
Acribel	2.5	3.1
Acrilan B 16	1.7	1.4
Acrilan B 57	3.2	1.4
Acrilan B 71 W	1.4	1.1
Acrilan flame-retarding	2.5	2.4
Beslon WD	3.2	2.6
Beslon WL	2.6	2.7
Cashmilon FW	3.6	2.0
Courtelle (dyed at pH 3.6)	1.8	2.3
Courtelle (dyed at pH 4.5)	3.2	3.4
Creslan T61	2.5	1.8
Creslan T 67	2.8	1.8
Crylor 50	1.3	2.1
Dolan Type 20	1.6	2.7
Dolan Type 22	3.0	2.7
Dralon	1.7	2.1
Exlan DK	4.6	2.1
Orlon 42	2.0	2.2
Orlon 75	2.0	2.3
Toraylon F	3.5	2.3
Vonnel V 17	2.3	1.3

TABLE 6.3

Dyeing Characteristics of Selected Basic Dyes

C.I. Generic Name C.I. Basic	CV value	f value
Yellow 28	3.0	0.26
Yellow 63	2.5	0.09
Red 46	3.0	0.43
Red 18	2.5	0.78
Red 15	3.0	0.29
Red 24	3.0	0.76
Blue 41	3.0	0.22
Blue 47	3.0	0.29
Blue 3	3.5	0.24
Blue 141	3.0	0.25
Astrazone Navy GSW (Bayer)	3.0	0.4
Astrazone Black SW (Bayer)	3.0	0.4

6.2.5 Dyeing techniques

The additions to the dyebath are thus as follows:

x% retarder, by calculation
2% acetic acid (80%), to give a pH of 4.0
0.5% EDTA, sequestering agent.

The following application technique is typical. The loaded yarn frame is entered into the machine which is filled with hot water (50°C), the temperature is raised as rapidly as possible to 80°C, the dyes and chemicals being added as the temperature is being raised. The bath is circulated at 80°C for 10 minutes, the temperature is then raised to 100°C at 0.25°C per minute and dyeing continued for 30 minutes. When on shade, the liquor is cooled to 55°C at a rate of 1.5°C per minute and dropped. When dye additions are to be made, the bath is cooled to 80°C, the dye added, and the heating cycle is repeated.

It is usual to dye acrylic packages with one-way flow only — in the 'in' to 'out' direction.

With the high level of exhaustion which can be obtained with basic dyes on acrylic fibres, and the resultant high degree of reproducibility, as well as with good control of the process as outlined in earlier chapters, it is possible to achieve 85—95% "blind", i.e. no-addition, dyeings.

It has been long recognized that an empirical relationship exists between package density, flow rate and constant rate of temperature rise (RAMP) with regard to the levelness of the dyeing obtained. For acrylic yarns, the following parameters have been considered satisfactory:

> package density, 350—400 g/l;
> flow rate, 40 l/kg/min;
> RAMP, 0.25° C/min.

Recently a systematic study was made [8] of these parameters and their influence on level dyeing of acrylic packages. This has enabled a series of matrices to be constructed from which the values of the three parameters can be read off for satisfactory results. Thus, with a flow rate of 35 l/kg/min and a package density of 350 g/l, level results will be obtained with any RAMP up to 0.3°C/min. As flow rate increases with constant density, the RAMP can also be increased. This work also showed the importance of the rate of exhaustion per circulation of liquor in determining the degree of unlevelness.

The profile for a typical dyeing process is shown in Figure 6.2.

Rapid-dyeing methods have been developed for acrylic fibre yarns, and one such recent development is the Alcosist CTL (Allied Colloids) Process. Selection of dyes for this process is on the same basis as that described earlier, but the retarder ensures that dye is virtually totally restrained from the fibre until the bath reaches the boil. This makes the process ideally suited for use when close control of temperature is not possible and for use on machines with poor circulation. Additions, if required, can be made at the boil.

Preferably, dyes of CV value 2.5—3.5 are used and the dye concentration value is calculated as before (i.e. % dye × f factor for each dye). This figure is then used to read off the amount of retarder required from a previously-prepared graph. An example of the graph is shown in Figure 6.3.

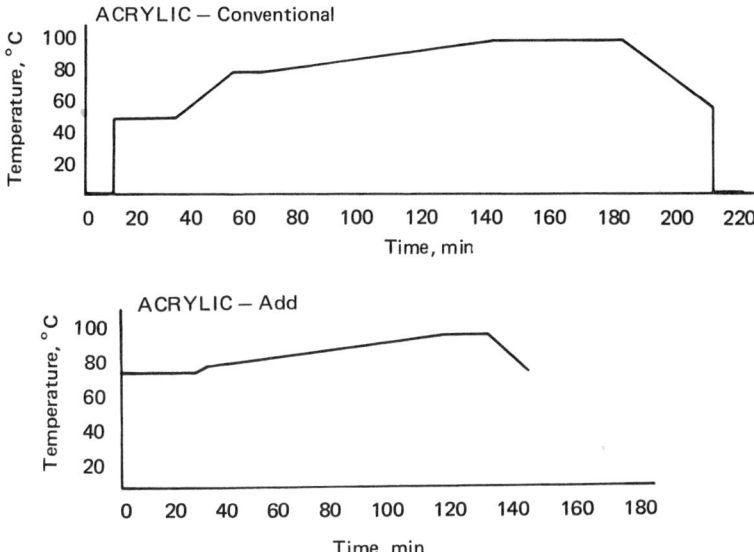

Figure 6.2 — Profile of a typical acrylic dyeing process

The temperature profile of this process, which has been used satisfactorily in bulk, is shown in Figure 6.4.

The yarn is entered into the machine and the dyebath is prepared at 60 to 70°C with:

x% Alcosist CTL (as calculated)
Acetic acid to give pH of 4
Softening agent.

The liquor is circulated while raising the temperature to 85°C, the dye added and circulation continued for a further 10 minutes. The temperature is then raised as rapidly as possible to the boil and circulation continued for 30 to 60 minutes. The bath is then cooled as described above. For shading additions, the quantities of retarder required are given in Table 6.4.

TABLE 6.4

Quantities of Alcosist CTL % for Shading

Fibre	0.01–0.5	*Depth of original shade (%)* 0.5 –2.0	2.0 –5.0
Slow strike	0.3 –0.6	0.25–0.5	0.2 –0.4
Medium strike	0.5 –0.8	0.35–0.7	0.3 –0.5
Rapid strike	0.7 –1.0	0.5 –0.8	0.35–0.6

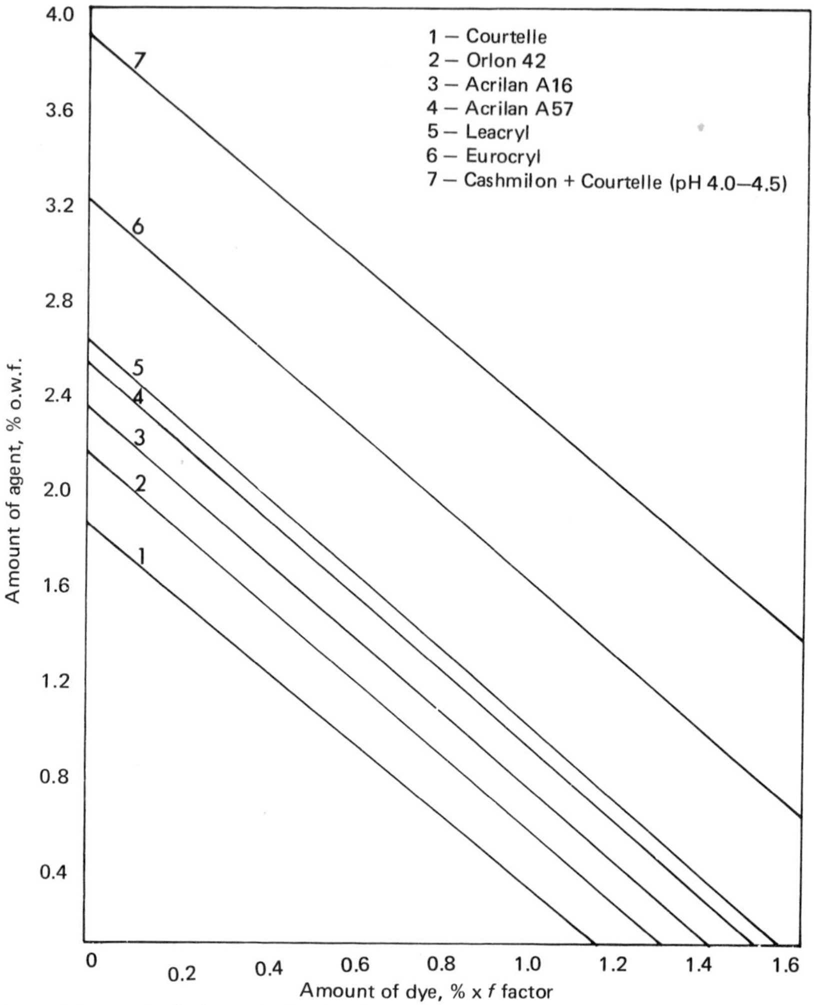

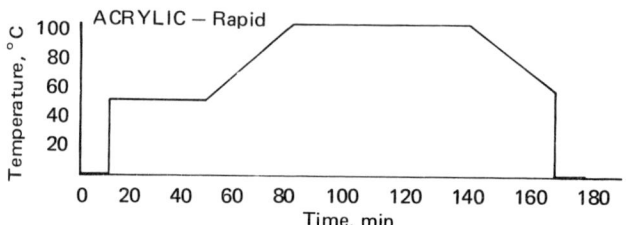

Figure 6.3 – Calculation of Alcosist CTL

Figure 6.4 – Alcosist CTL rapid-dyeing process

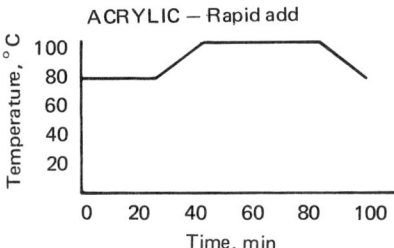

Figure 6.5 — Profile of shading procedure for the rapid-dyeing process

6.2.6 Basic dye selection

A large range of shades can be obtained with a three-colour combination of CV3 dyes such as:

    C.I. Basic Yellow 28,
    C.I. Basic Red 46 and
    C.I. Basic Blue 41.

These dyes can be augmented by a further small range of CV3 dyes to obtain bright shades or hues not obtainable by using the ternary mixture. These dyes have already been listed in Table 6.3, but the various end uses for which they are suitable are detailed in Table 6.5. In general the dyes have a high level of wet fastness and only minor changes in the selection are necessary when higher light fastness is demanded, such as for furnishing fabrics or carpets, or when minimum cross-staining is required for the dyeing of blended yarns.

For automotive end uses, the following dyes can be used on dry spun fibres to obtain adequate light fastness:

    C.I. Basic Yellow 21, 28*, 63.
    C.I. Basic Orange 28.
    C.I. Basic Red 18*, 24, 25, 78.
    C.I. Basic Blue 45 and Blue 47* (for heavy shades only).
    * basis for blacks.

With mixture yarns, the retarder is calculated to allow for the acrylic portion of the blend. Blends with wool or cellulosic fibres are generally package dyed with only the acrylic component being coloured. Cross-staining of the wool or nylon can be further minimized by dyeing at pH 4, with the temperature at or above the boil and using the minimum of dyebath auxiliaries. A special method for dyeing solid shades, principally on wool-rich acrylic blends, will be discussed later. With carpet yarns, since fibre denier and yarn count are generally coarser than with hosiery yarns, a relatively faster RAMP can be employed. With yarns produced from modified acrylic fibres (e.g. Teklan S), 20 g/l of common salt is added to the dyebath and the temperature should not exceed 94°C during dyeing to avoid delustring.

Modified acrylic fibres are increasing in importance as the requirements for non-flammable textile materials become more stringent. For end uses such as furnishing fabrics, a light fastness of 6 is often required. The following dyes will give a minimum light fastness of 6 at all depths.

> C.I. Basic Yellow 19, 21, 25, 28, 49, 59 and 63
> Orange 36
> Red 22, 29
> Blue 54, 78.

The following dyes are recommended as a trichromatic combination*:

> Basacryl Yellow 5RL (BASF) (C.I. Basic Yellow 25)
> Basacryl Red GL   (BASF) (C.I. Basic Red 29)
> Basacryl Blue GGL   (BASF) (C.I. Basic Blue 78)
> *For this application, it has been found that *Colour Index* equivalents are
> not always satisfactory.

As mentioned earlier, CV 1 dyes may be useful in certain cases and a suitable trichromatic combination which will obtain a wide gamut of shades is:

> C.I. Basic Orange 42
> Red 45
> Blue 69.

6.2.7 Soft finish

Soft finishes are normally applied to acrylic yarns to improve the handle and knitting characteristics. These can be applied with the dye, in the cooling bath or in a fresh bath. Current practice is to use a permanent finish which will withstand 6—10 domestic washes. These products are best applied in the dyebath, when up to 2% of products such as Alcamine PF (Allied Colloids) are used.

6.2.8 Dispensing

Basic dyes are dispensed by pasting with acetic acid and then dissolved in about 40 times their weight of nearly boiling water (*do not boil*). Using dispense tanks, three separate additions are often required. The acetic acid and chemicals are mixed and delivered first, then the soft finish, the dye being dispensed to the dyeing vessel last.

6.2.9 Scouring

Certain yarns with high levels of contaminants, such as spin finishes, may require a detergent scour using 1% agent (o.w.f.) at $50^{\circ}C$ for 10 minutes, before dyeing.

TABLE 6.5

Dyes for Acrylic Yarns

Dye or C.I. Generic Name	Usage	Suitability for						
		Normal acrylic end use	Furnishing	Carpets	Modacrylic	Blends with wool	Blends with nylon	Blends with cotton
C.I. Basic								
Yellow 28	Trichromatic component	✓	✓	✓	✓	✓	✓	✓
Yellow 63	Bright shades (emerald, turq.)	✓			✓	✓	✓	✓
Red 46	Trichromatic component	✓	✓	✓	✓	✓	✓	✓
Red 18	Alternative tertiary component	✓	✓	✓	✓	✓	✓	✓
Red 15	For pinks	✓	✓	✓		✓	✓	✓
Red 24	Maroons, burgundies	✓	✓✓	✓✓		✓✓	✓✓	✓✓
Blue 41	Trichromatic component	✓	✓✓	✓✓	✓✓	✓✓	✓✓	✓✓
Blue 47	For red flare	✓	✓	✓	✓	✓	✓	✓
Blue 3	For turquoises		✓	✓	✓✓	✓		
Blue 141	For turquoises				✓			
Mixture Navy such as Astrazone Navy GSW (Bayer)	For navies	✓	✓	✓✓		✓✓	✓✓	✓
Mixture Black such as Astrazone Black SW (Bayer)	For blacks	✓	✓	✓		✓	✓	✓

6.2.10 Correction of faulty dyeings

Basic dyes can be levelled by running the dyed material at 104°C for 90 minutes in for example:—

> 2.5% Migrassist ACD (Tanatex)
> 2.0% Sulphuric acid (96%)

Some dye can be stripped by treating at 104°C for 60 minutes with e.g. 3 g/l Lyogen AS (Sandoz). An alternative method for stripping is to use 5 g/l soap at the boil, but this method is not so effective in package dyeing.

6.2.11 Whites

Whites are normally obtained by using a simple application of a fluorescent whitening agent. The following routine is typical:

> x% cationic FWA (such as 0.3% Blankophor DBS 8OR (Bayer))
> 1.0 g/l EDTA
> Acetic acid 80% to pH 4.0
> 2.0% Diphasol OC (CGY)
>
> Start at 60°C, raise to 98°C at 1.5°C/min
> Run 20 minutes
> Cool to 60°C
> Warm rinse
> Soften in a fresh bath

If the untreated fibre is cream-coloured, a more extensive treatment may be required:

> x% cationic FWA
> 0.5 g/l Oxalic acid
> 0.125 g/l Sodium bisulphite
> 1.5 g/l EDTA
> 2.0% Diphasol OC (CGY)
> 0.25 g/l Calgon T (Albright - Wilson) — to be added last, when the temperature is at least 70°C
> Raise to 98°C at 1.5°C/min
> Run 20 minutes
> Cool to 60°C
> Warm rinse — Soften in fresh bath
> NOTE: the sequestering agents will eliminate about 12 p.p.m. hardness

For an exceptionally high quality white, which is not subject to wet fading, an extensive, three-stage process based on a chlorite bleach followed by FWA application is required. The details of the process are given below:

(a)   2 g/l Sodium chlorite liq.
              formic acid to pH 4.0

              Set bath at 60° C, add chemicals, check pH (4.0)
              Raise to 90° C at 3° C/min
              Raise from 90° C to 98° C at 0.25° C/min
              Run 20 minutes
              Cool to 60° C

(b)   Rinse at 40° C for 5 minutes

(c)   Antichlor — 20 minutes at 60° C using:

              2 g/l Sodium bicarbonate
              2 g/l Sodium metabisulphite

(d)   Rinse at 40° C for 5 minutes

(e) x% cationic FWA

              0.5 g/l E.D.T.A.
              2.0% Diphasol OC (CGY)

              Set bath at 60° C, raise to 90° C at 0.5° C/min
              Run 40 minutes
              Cool 60° C

(f)   Rinse at 40° C for 5 minutes

(g)   Rinse at 40° C for 5 minutes

(h)   Soften in fresh bath

With all white processes, soft finish is applied in a fresh bath. Cationic FWAs are preferred since they are more compatible with the soft finishes employed.

6.2.12 Acrylic yarns — special precautions for hank processing

The principal method of dyeing acrylic yarn in hank form is with basic dyes, using those of CV value 3. The methods are essentially the same as those described for package processing, but two modifications are worth consideration:

— the use of Alcosist CTL as the retarder system, since this ensures that the dye is virtually totally restrained until the dyebath reaches the boil. Slow adsorption of the dye then occurs, which makes the system ideal for machines with poor circulation or when temperature control equipment is not available. Additions can also be made at the boil;

— the use of lower rates of temperature rise, for example, $0.1-0.25^\circ$ C per minute. This can be readily achieved in computer-controlled machines. A temperature-pause method can also be used.

Other possibilities which might prove beneficial when dyeing acrylic yarns in hank form include:

— the use of disperse dyes in pale shades, although some reduction in reproducibility might need to be accepted;
— the use of CV5 basic dyes for pale-to-medium shades. These are applied by the normal retarder techniques and a suitable trichromatic combination is:

C.I. Basic Orange 29
C.I. Basic Red 22 and
C.I. Basic Blue 22.

— the use of the so-called 'migrating' basic dyes [2], such as the Maxilon M (Ciba—Geigy) or Remacryl E (Hoechst) dyes.

The method for applying Maxilon M dyes is as follows. The bath is prepared at 80°C with:

2% Acetic acid (80%) to give pH 4.0
1% Sodium acetate
10% Sodium sulphate anhydrous

plus the dye and the retarder. The loaded hank frame is lowered into the machine, the bath brought to the boil in 15 minutes and this temperature maintained for 60 minutes. Shading additions can be made at the boil.

The amount of the retarder, Tinegal MR (Ciba—Geigy), which is required is given by the simple expression:

% Tinegal MR = 0.5 — % dye

Acrylic yarns require to be cooled slowly before removal from the machine after dyeing, so that machines with cooling coils are best suited for these yarns. Other fibre types can generally be cooled simply by dropping the dyebath and filling with cold water with a consequent saving in water, provided that the exhaust liquors are not fed directly to the sewer.

6.3 POLYESTER YARNS

Both continuous filament (CF) and staple polyester yarns are dyed in package form with disperse dyes, preferably at 130—135°C, without carriers since certain of these products can reduce fastness, especially to light, and others are ecologically undesirable. In general, little polyester, either alone or in blends, is dyed in hank form.

6.3.1 Conventional application technique

The yarn is placed in the machine, which is filled with hot water, and the temperature raised to 75°C. Circulation is in the 'in' to 'out' direction only, on maximum speed (usually about 60 litres/kg/minute) and a small amount of anti-foaming agent is added. The dyebath is prepared with:

> 1.0% Dispersing agent, such as Alcosperse BT (Allied Colloids)
> Acetic acid to give pH of 5
> 0.5 g/l EDTA

When the temperature has reached 75°C, the flow is changed to 'out' to 'in', and the dyes and chemicals added. The direction/time pattern is changed to 3 minutes in each direction and the temperature raised to 135°C at 1°C per minute and maintained at this temperature for 45 minutes.

The bath is then cooled to 75°C before being dropped, if high-temperature drains are not provided.

6.3.2 Rapid-dyeing method

When high flow rates are possible, a rapid-dyeing technique may be used. The machine and dyebath are prepared as described above, but the dye is added, using the flow sequence 5 minutes 'out' to 'in', 5 minutes 'in' to 'out', etc. The flow is then changed to 'out' to 'in' and maintained in this direction while the temperature is raised to 135°C at the maximum rate of rise. When the top temperature is reached, the flow is reversed every three minutes and circulation continued for 45 minutes. Cool, etc., as above.

Sophisticated processes for rapid dyeing have been developed, of which an outstanding example is the Resolin S process [3]. This depends on:

- calculating the optimum starting temperature
- determining the temperature range during which dye goes on the fibre
- using the RAMP, or carrier amount, which gives optimum dyeing results
- determining the time at top temperature to ensure adequate penetration.

Technical restrictions on the selection of dyes can limit the usefulness of such procedures. The success of the process depends on knowing the dyeing rate of the dyes, the affinity of the polyester yarn and the characteristics of the dyeing machine.

6.3.3 Reduction clearing

The fastness properties of deep dyeings can be improved by reduction clearing in a fresh bath for 20 minutes at 80°C with; for example:

Sodium hydroxide flake	2 g/l
Sodium hydrosulphite	3 g/l
Alcosperse BT (Allied Colloids)	1 g/l

The machine is drained and the yarn rinsed in a bath containing 1 g/l formic acid.

6.3.4 Levelling

Unlevel dyeings can be corrected in a bath containing, for example:

> 0.5% Acetic acid (80%)
> 3 g/l Chemocarrier LHN (Tanatex)

The bath is prepared at 70°C, the temperature raised to 130°C at 1°C per minute and treatment continued for 60 minutes. After cooling the bath, the yarn is rinsed and a reduction-clearing treatment may be required. 'Non-carrier' levelling agents, such as Rexan SRO—5 (Dexter), can be used, since they are less likely to affect the light-fastness properties.

6.3.5 Oligomers

A common problem in the dyeing of polyester materials is the liberation of oligomer, particularly cyclic trimers, from the material during high-temperature treatment. These can be deposited on the surface of yarns, machines and in the pumps. The incidence of oligomer problems can be minimized by:

- avoiding the use of carriers
- minimum treatments at high temperature
- dropping of dyeing liquors at high temperatures.

Certain processes have been developed to minimize oligomer deposition. One such process, which has been found satisfactory in use, is that based on System PPD (Rowan Palm). Other similar systems include Dilatin 7504E (Sandoz) and Product 1193 (Hoechst). The main purpose of these systems is to keep both yarn and machinery clean.

6.3.6 The System PPD technique

The technique depends on the use of:

> 0.5% Acetic acid (80%)
> 3.0% System PPD (Rowan Palm)

The yarn is entered into the machine which is filled with hot water and the temperature raised as rapidly as possible to 70°C. The dyes and chemicals are added and the temperature raised from 70 to 130°C at 1°C per minute. The machine is run at this temperature for 30—60 minutes, depending on shade. Circulation throughout is two-way, 3 minutes in each direction.

The contents of the machine are cooled as rapidly as possible to 80°C for draining. Reduction clearing is only necessary for very heavy shades and it has been found that, in a typical shade range, where 40% of shades required to be reduction cleared, only 5% required this treatment when the System PPD was used. 1.5% Lubricant TCA (Rowan Palm) a lubricant—oligomer binder, may be applied in the last rinse bath for 20 minutes in the cold. When using this procedure the machine must first be boiled out with System PPD to avoid contamination of the yarn.

Dyeing profiles of the above processes are shown in Figure 6.6.

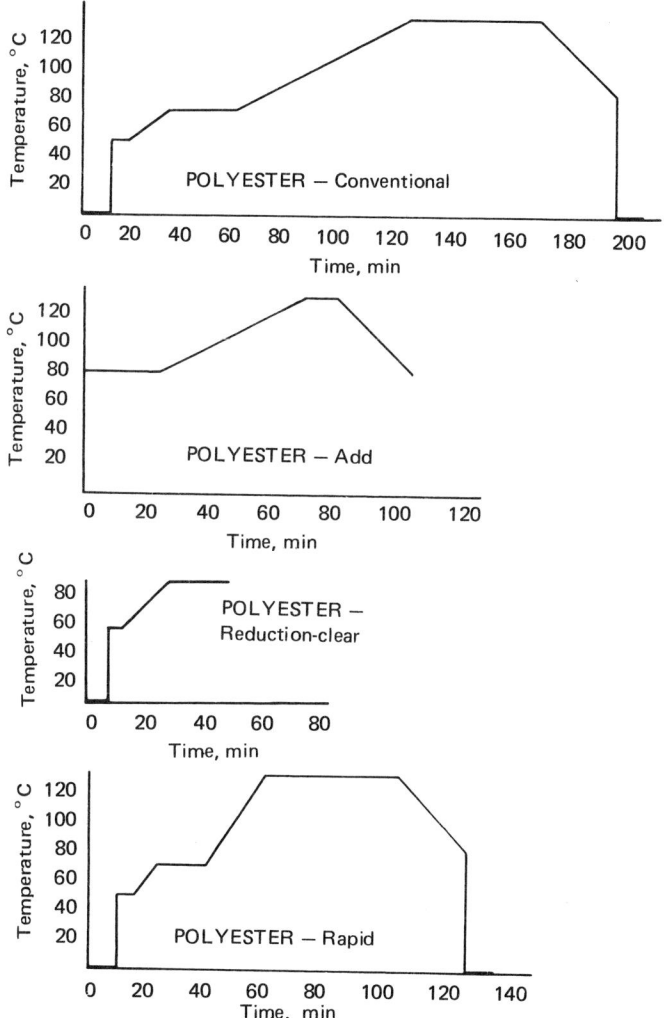

Figure 6.6 – Polyester dyeing methods

6.3.7 Knit–de-knit (KDK)

Rolls of KDK fabric, loaded on spindles, may be dyed by either the conventional or System PPD method, but the RAMP is reduced to 0.5°C per minute.

6.3.8 Staple Yarns

The methods given above are applicable to both CF and staple yarns. Certain staple yarns, such as the ICI Type 556 yarn, take up dye rapidly and so the procedure is modified. The yarn is entered, the bath prepared at 60°C, and the dyes and chemicals added. The temperature is raised from 60 to 90°C at 0.25°C per minute, the machine run for 15 minutes, then the temperature raised to 130°C at 0.25°C per minute and the dyeing continued for 30 minutes. The flow is reversed as before.

6.3.9 Dye selection

Disperse dyes for polyester are normally classified, for example, by ICI, as A to D types [4]. C and D dyes, which show high fastness to sublimation, are often used for package dyeing. If liquid brands are used, larger amounts of dispersing agent must be added to the dyebath, since liquids contain less dispersing agent than powder brands. It is often necessary to select dyes according to manufacturer, rather than on the basis of *Colour Index* equivalents, since disperse dyes which have the same chemical constitution may vary widely in their dispersion stability during dyeing. Selection of dyes for polyester yarn dyeing is largely covered by three groupings (see below).

6.3.9.1 Dyes for Texturised Yarns, e.g. for Double Jersey Fabric

These dyes, in addition to being fast to normal end-use agencies, such as light, washing, perspiration and rubbing, require to be fast to stentering at temperatures up to 180°C. This means that dyes with a high sublimation fastness must be used, and this can be difficult to achieve in full shades. Many selections are possible, but a typical and satisfactory selection is given in Table 6.6.

TABLE 6.6

Disperse Dyes on Polyester Yarn for Double Jersey End Use

Dye	Classification	Use
C.I. Disperse Yellow 126	D	Bright shades
Orange 54	C	Trichromatic component
Orange 13	C	''
Orange 25	B	Bright oranges
Red 60	B	Pale shades
Violet 33	C	Heavy reds
Red 82	C	''
Blue 297	C	Navies
Violet 57		Violet shades
Blue 87	C	Turquoises
Blue 56	B	Pale shades
Mixture Black such as Dispersol Black D2B (ICI)	D	Blacks

6.3.9.2 Fast to Cross-dyeing against White Nylon

The main end use for these yarns is to create coloured effects in nylon half-hose. Yarn dyed with these dyes is required to give no staining when plaited with an equal weight of white nylon and treated in a bath containing 4% formic acid for 1 hour at 85°C. When normal application methods are used, a double reduction-clearing may be necessary with full shades. Using the System PPD method, only one reduction-clear may be necessary, even for the heaviest shades.
One suitable dye selection is given in Table 6.7.

TABLE 6.7

Disperse Dyes on Polyester Fast to Cross-dyeing

C.I. Disperse Yellow 64
Orange 13
Red 11 (in pale shades)
Red 82
Violet 35
Blue 79
Blue 87
Mixture Black such as
Dispersol Black D–2B (ICI)

6.3.9.3 Dyes for Automotive Yarns

The main criteria for dye selection are high fastness to light at elevated temperatures and to heat treatments which may be encountered in subsequent stentering, heat setting or laminating. The dyes are applied by the conventional method in the presence of dilute acid and dispersing agent. A nucleus of suitable dyes is given in Table 6.8.

TABLE 6.8

Disperse Dyes on Polyester for Automotive End Use

C.I. Disperse Yellow 42
Orange 30
Red 86.1
Blue 56 (in pale shades)
Blue 87
Blue 73 (for navies, etc.)
Violet 57 (to correct metamerism)

6.3.9.4 Coverage of Barré

Variations in the dyeability of CF polyester yarns may occur due to physical differences introduced into the yarn as a result of non-uniform conditions during previous thermal treatments, or tension differences in processes such as texturizing. Careful dye selection will assist in overcoming this problem, but, due to the high fastness demands made on dyed yarns, it is seldom possible to select dyes purely on the basis of their ability to give dyeings free from barriness (barré).

6.3.9.5 Compatibility

As has been discussed earlier, use of compatible mixtures of dyes leads to significant improvements in level dyeing. It is difficult to select an entirely compatible mixture of disperse dyes, and this is not assisted by the stringent fastness requirements which have to be met. Recent work [5] has led to a method of dye selection according to a compatibility number (V). The compatibility number is related to the time of half dyeing $(t_{1/2})$ according to the equation:

$$V = \frac{70 - t_{1/2}}{10}$$

It has been found that a compatible mixture at one depth and in one set of proportions may not be so at others, so that this can lead to an increase in the number of dyes which must be stocked. Fastness restrictions may mean that there is no alternative but to use incompatible mixtures.

The so-called 'non-carrier' type of levelling agent can be useful in promoting level dyeing in cases where the fastness restrictions placed on dyes means that incompatible mixtures must be used. The use of 2 g/l Palegal SF (BASF), which is stated to be a 'synchronizing' agent, improves compatibility and allows a more rapid rise in temperature. This product has no effect on light fastness, exerts a retarding effect up to 100 to 110°C and, above this temperature, promotes migration.

6.3.9.6 Dispensing

This has been described in Section 6.2.1.

6.3.9.7 Whites

These are obtained using an FWA e.g. Palanil Brilliant White R (BASF), a typical recipe being:

> 0.2% Palanil Brilliant White R (BASF)
> 1% Acetic acid (80%)
> 0.5% EDTA
> 2% Dispersing agent

Treatment is for 45 minutes at 130°C.

6.4 NYLON (POLYAMIDE) YARNS

Nylon yarns, both staple and continuous filament, are generally dyed in package form with acid and 1:2 metal-complex dyes to obtain the necessary fastness on yarns for weaving, knitting and carpets. In hank, nylon yarns can be dyed with the equalising acid, acid milling and 1:2 metal - complex dyes selected for package dyeing. Greater use is likely to be made of the level-dyeing properties of monosulphonated acid dyes, such as the Tectilon (Ciba—Geigy) range (see 6.4.1). Hand-knitting and carpet yarns are widely dyed in hank form, but yarn for many end uses, especially automotive fabrics and machine-knitting yarns, cannot be dyed in this form because the high fastness required can only be achieved using dyes with poor level-dyeing properties.

When dyeing either nylon or wool with such dyes, it is usual practice to employ a levelling agent. These are of two principal types:

(a) *anionic agents,* which have affinity for the fibre and act as blocking agents, being slowly released to allow dye to enter the fibre as dyeing proceeds. Lyogen P (Sandoz) is a well-known example of this type;

(b) *cationic—nonionic agents,* which form complexes with the dyes. These complexes break down and the dye is liberated slowly as the temperature of the bath is increased. Examples of this type of agent include Albegal SW (Ciba—Geigy) and Sandogen NH (Sandoz).

The main types of nylon encountered are nylon 6.6 and nylon 6. The details given in the following sections have been selected with Nylon 6.6 principally in mind. Nylon 6 is more rapid dyeing and may require a slower RAMP than nylon 6.6. The light and wet fastness properties of certain dyes may also be slightly lower on nylon 6.

As will be mentioned again later, barré dyeing can be a problem with nylon due to variations in chemical or physical properties arising from the previous history of the material. Thermal treatment of the fibre may also cause changes in rates of dyeing, but this problem can usually be overcome by adjusting the rate of temperature rise during dyeing, together with control of pH.

6.4.1 Monosulphonated equalising acid dyes

A small number of these dyes have been found useful for dyeing continuous filament carpet yarn, and will give adequate fastness for that particular end use up to about 2% depth. The dyes are applied with for example:

> 2% Novanyl Leveller A L (YCL)
> 1% Ammonium sulphate to give pH of 6.5 or
> Acetic acid (80%) to give pH 5.5.

Dyeing is commenced at 40°C, the temperature raised to the boil at 1°C per minute and the dyeing continued for 30 minutes. When additions are made, the bath is first cooled to 40°C. Suitable dyes are given in Table 6.9.

TABLE 6.9

Monosulphonated Dyes for Nylon

Tectilon	Yellow 4R	)		(C.I. Acid Yellow 219)
	Red 2B200	)	Ternary combination	(C.I. Acid Red 361)
	Blue 4R	)		(C.I. Acid Blue 277)
	Yellow 10M	)		
		)	For bright greens, etc.	
	Blue 6G	)		(C.I. Acid Blue 258)

6.4.2 Acid Milling Dyes

With these dyes, dyeing is commenced at 40°C in a bath containing, for example:

2% Sandogen NH (Sandoz)
3% Ammonium sulphate
Acetic acid to adjust the pH to 6 to 6.5

The temperature is raised to 100°C at 1°C per minute and dyeing continued for 30 minutes to exhaust the bath. The bath is cooled to 40°C prior to making additions and the yarn must be well rinsed before aftertreatments.

6.4.3 Aftertreatment

The wet fastness of acid dyes on nylon is improved by aftertreatment with either a syntan or by a full back-tan treatment.

6.4.3.1 Syntan

After dyeing and rinsing, the fresh bath is made up cold with 2% formic acid, and the yarn is treated in it for 5 minutes, after which e.g. 3% Alcofix PA (Allied Colloids) is added. The temperature is raised to 65°C in 20 minutes and treatment continued for 20 minutes, after which the bath is dropped and the yarn is given two cold rinses.

6.4.3.2 Full Back-tanning

After dyeing and rinsing, the fresh bath is prepared containing:

2% Tannic acid and
2% Formic acid (85%)

at 70°C; the yarn is treated in it for 20 minutes and the bath drained. The yarn is then treated with 1% tartar emetic in a fresh bath at 70°C for 20 minutes, the bath drained and the yarn then given a hot, followed by a cold rinse.

6.4.4 1:2 metal-complex dyes

Dyeing is commenced at 40°C in a bath containing, for example:

> 3% Ammonium sulphate
> Acetic acid to give a pH of 6 to 6.5
> 1.5% Avolan IWF (Bayer)

The temperature is raised to 100°C at 1°C per minute and dyeing continued at 100°C for 30 minutes to obtain exhaustion. If shading additions are required the bath is cooled to 40°C before these are made. The yarn is rinsed well after dyeing.

The time/temperature profiles of the dyeing cycles for nylon are shown in Figure 6.7. It has been found that Avolan IWF (Bayer), in addition to its levelling properties, possesses good dispersion properties for use in package dyeing and if an agent of this type is not used, poor rubbing fastness can result when metal-complex dyes are applied.

A novel development is the Sandacid V technique (Sandoz) which can be used with high-fastness dyes that are otherwise difficult to apply, especially to physically-variable materials. For example, this method is useful for dyeing automotive yarns, using the dyes cited in Section 6.4.6. The mode of action of this agent is to lower the pH gradually by hydrolysis in the bath to liberate acid as dyeing proceeds, so that slow absorption of the dyes takes place. The outline of the process is as follows.

The yarn is pretreated for 5 minutes at 50°C with:

> 1% Sandogen NH
> Soda ash to give pH of 9.0

The dye is added, the temperature of the bath raised to 100°C at 1.5°C per minute and treatment continued for 10 minutes. 0.25 g/l Sandacid V is added and dyeing is continued for a further 30 minutes to obtain exhaustion.

6.4.4.1 Dissolving

Acid milling, 1:2 metal-complex and chrome dyes (see Section 6.5.3) are pasted with cold water, nearly boiling water is added until the dyes are completely dissolved. The mixture is added to the dispensing tank and stirred.

6.4.5 Dye selection

A small range of acid milling and 1:2 metal-complex dyes can be used on nylon, wool and blended yarns. This selection is given in Table 6.10. It can be seen that a relatively small number of 17 dyes from the two classes is sufficient for a wide range of fibre types to be dyed for a variety of end uses.

Barré dyeing can be a problem with nylon due to both chemical and physical variations in the substrate, particularly the latter. It is possible to reduce the risk by dye selection, but difficulties may arise due to the fastness requirements demanded. Pretreatment with agents such as Univadine MC (CGY) can reduce the problem, but products of this type can be dye selective. Careful control of pH is another method of dealing with the problem.

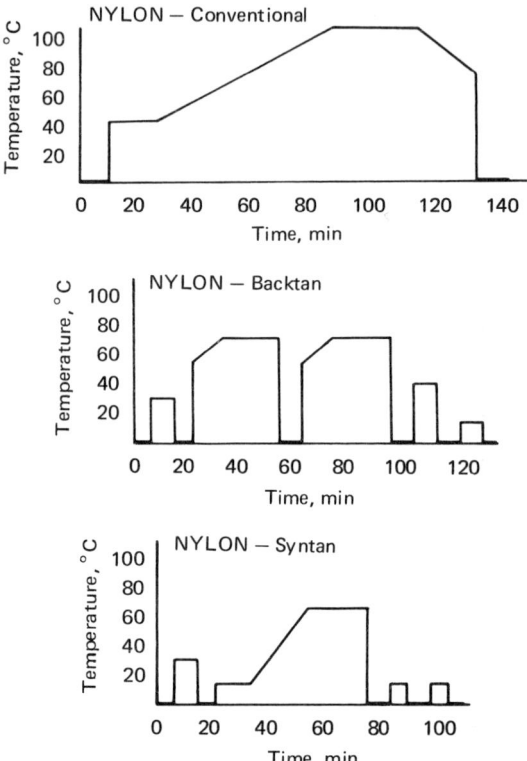

Figure 6.7 — Dyeing profiles for nylon

6.4.6 Nylon automotive yarns

Nylon used for this end use often contains a 'light-protective' agent to prevent fibre degradation on exposure to sun light. Even so, the dyes used for automotive yarns must not only give high light fastness but must not themselves promote photochemical degradation. Dye selection is therefore difficult. Further, dyes which are satisfactory when used alone give inferior results in certain mixtures if catalytic fading occurs. Individual mixture dyeings must therefore be tested. A suitable dye selection is given in Table 6.11.

TABLE 6.10

Selection of Acid Milling and 1:2 Metal-complex Dyes for Nylon and Wool

	Nylon CF and Staple	Wool-Hosiery, Carpets, Wool Blends	Wool—Nylon
Acid Milling			
C.I. Acid Yellow 79	✓	✓	✓
Red 111	✓	✓	✓
Violet 48	✓	✓	✓
Red 134	✓	✓	✓
Blue 247	✓		
Blue 138	✓	✓	✓
Green 25	✓	✓	✓
Nylomine Black CR	✓		
Blue 80		✓	
1:2 Metal-complex Dyes			
C.I. Acid Yellow 121	✓	✓	✓
Orange 144	✓	✓	✓
Red 359	✓	✓	✓
Black 211	✓	✓	✓
Blue 284	✓	✓	✓
Brown 365	✓	✓	
Green 108	✓	✓	✓
Isolan Grey PR LE 200		✓	

TABLE 6.11

Dyes for Automotive Nylon Yarns

Neutrichrome Yellow S—JR LL (C.I. Acid Yellow 121)
Lanasyn Yellow 2R L (C.I. Acid Orange 80)
Neutrichrome Red S—JL (in full shades only) (C.I. Acid Red 359)
Lanasyn Red 2GLN (for shading component only) (C.I. Acid Red 216)
Avilon Scarlet 2R (C.I. Acid Red 316)
Irgalan Blue FBL
Isolan Green PR LE
Lanasyn Dark Brown S—GL (C.I. Acid Brown 298)
Telon Fast Black LD (C.I. Acid Black 172)

The dyeing method, except for blacks, is to commence dyeing at $40°C$ in a bath containing:

> 1% Sandogen NH
> 2% Ammonium sulphate
> Acetic acid to give pH 5.5 for full shades,
>   pH 6.5 for pale shades
> An anionic blocking agent — such as
> Univadine MC — is useful to assist in
> covering barriness

The temperature is raised to 100°C at 1°C per minute and the dyeing continued for 30 minutes, if necessary for exhaustion.

For blacks, the bath is prepared at 40°C with:

> 3% Ammonium sulphate
> Acetic acid to give pH of 5.0

The dyeing procedure is as above, but acetic acid to give pH of 3.5 can be added to promote exhaustion, if necessary.

When required, wet fastness can be improved by the application of a syntan.

6.4.7 Differential-dyeing nylon

The popularity of differential-dyeing effects has declined in recent years and little was produced by the yarn-dyeing route in any case. However, intermingled carpet yarns, containing differential-dyeing components, have been produced by the fibre suppliers, and these can be dyed in package form.

Dyeing is commenced at pH 5.5 and at 40°C, raising the temperature to 100°C at 0.5°C per minute. Dyeing at this temperature should not exceed 30 minutes. A possible short selection of trichromatic mixtures is given in Table 6.12.

TABLE 6.12

Dyes for Differential-dyeing Nylon

Dyes which will dye all components equally	Dyes for acid dyeing components	Dyes for basic dyeing component
C.I. Disperse Yellow 3	C.I. Acid Yellow 219	C.I. Basic Yellow 45
Red 55	Red 361	Red 60
Blue 7	Blue 277	Blue 22

6.4.8 Whites

These are normally obtained by applying FWAs, the following recipe being typical:

> 1.5% Blankophor CL liquid (Bayer)
> Acetic acid to give pH of 4.5
> 1% EDTA

treatment is continued for 30 minutes at 90°C.

6.4.9 Levelling of faulty dyeings

Levelling techniques for nylon depend on raising the dyebath pH to remove dye from the yarn, then re-applying the dye by slowly lowering the pH again. This process can be assisted by the use of levelling agents.

6.5 WOOL YARNS IN PACKAGE

Wool yarns, manufactured on a number of spinning systems, (for example, worsted, woollen, open-end) are dyed in package form. These yarns are preferably dry spun, that is with a minimum quantity of lubricant. Lubricants which are water-soluble and can be removed by a simple water rinse, or which will remain stable after removal in the dyebath, are preferred, since extensive scouring procedures for yarn in package form are expensive. In addition, total removal of lubricant, when present in high concentrations, is difficult, not least because of the filtering effect of the packages.

Yarns for weaving, knitting and carpets are dyed with acid milling and metal-complex dyes, since these dyes will give the consistent reproducibility that is required for the success of package dyeing and at the same time give the excellent fastness associated with these dyes. Although chrome dyes are less important than they were, largely due to effluent disposal problems, this class of dye is still used for navies and blacks, particularly if the so-called 'low-chrome' dyeing methods are used.

For yarns made from wool which has been given a shrink-resist treatment in the sliver stage, or for yarn to be so treated as fabric or garments, reactive dyes are used, supplemented by dyes from the ranges mentioned above.

6.5.1 Scouring

With water-soluble lubricants, a rinse in water at 70°C for 15 minutes will be sufficient. A more severe scour can be given using:

> 3% Sufatol LS3 (Standard Chemicals)
> 3% Soda ash

for 20 minutes at 65°C, followed by thorough rinsing.

6.5.2 Acid milling and 1:2 metal-complex dyes

The dyebath is prepared at 50°C, after loading the yarn, with, for example:

> Acetic acid to give pH of 5.5 to 6
> 2% Albegal SW (Ciba—Geigy), as levelling agent
> 0.3% Eulan WA new (Bayer), if mothproofing is required.

The temperature is raised to the boil at 1°C per minute, and dyeing continued for 30 minutes at the boil to obtain exhaustion, additional acetic acid being added, if necessary.

For shading additions, the bath is cooled to 70°C and the RAMP procedure is repeated. A warm and a cold rinse complete the process. Dye selection is given in Table 6.10.

6.5.3   Chrome dyes (e.g. Bayer low-chrome method)

The dyebath is prepared at 40°C with, for example:

> 3% Acetic acid (80%)
> 1% Formic acid (85%) to give pH 3.5 and
> 0.5% Alcosist PL (Allied Colloids)

The bath is circulated for 10 minutes, the dye added, the temperature raised to 100°C at 1.5°C per minute and circulation continued for a further 20 minutes. A further 1% formic acid (85%) is added to exhaust, if necessary, and dyeing is continued for a further 10 minutes. The bath is cooled to 75°C and potassium dichromate calculated as indicated in Table 6.11 is added. The temperature is raised to 100°C at a rate of 1.5°C per minute, 7.5% sodium sulphate is added and chroming continued at the boil for 15 minutes. The bath is then cooled and a cold rinse completes the process. The dyes used and the method of calculating the required amount of dichromate are given in Table 6.13.

TABLE 6.13

Chrome Dyes

Dye	GCr Factor	
Diamond Black PV 1 25%	0.15	(C.I. Mordant Black 9)
Diamond Navy Blue RRN	0.15	

Potassium dichromate requirement = % dye × GCr factor (summed for each dye in the recipe). Minimum of 0.25%.

6.5.4   Dyeing of Superwash wool

Reactive dyes are widely used for dyeing shrink-resisted yarns to meet Superwash (IWS) requirements. These dyes are also applicable to conventional wool yarns, if high wet fastness and bright shades are required.

Irrespective of dye class, yarn that has been given a previous anti-shrink treatment, is treated in cold water and the pH checked. Adjustment is made to pH 6.5 before commencing dyeing and in some cases no acid addition is required.

6.5.4.1   Reactive Dyes

Reactive dyes were initially developed and exploited for dyeing cellulosic fibres, but a number of ranges have been developed specifically for wool. The Lanasol range (Ciba—Geigy) is probably the one that has been most widely accepted and used, and the application of these dyes is described below. The various ranges of reactive dyes available for wool are reviewed in Table 6.14.

TABLE 6.14

Reactive Dye Ranges for Wool

Dye Name	Manufacturer	Reactive System	Year Developed
Remalan	Hoechst	vinyl sulphone and	
		β-sulphatoethylsulphone	1952
Remalan Fast E	"	β-sulphatoethylsulphone	1958
Cibacrolan	Ciba—Geigy	monochlorotriazine	1961
Drimalan	Sandoz	ω-chloroacetylamino	1962
Remazolan	Hoechst	β-sulphatoethylsulphone	1963
Procilan	ICI	acrylamido	1964
(Now withdrawn)			
Lanasol	Ciba—Geigy	α-bromoacrylamido	1966
Lanafix	Sumitomo	acrylamido and	
		β-sulphatoethylsulphone	1967
Verofix	Bayer)		
Drimalan F	Sandoz)	monochlorodifluoropyrimidine	1970
Reactolan	Geigy)		
(Now withdrawn)			
Hostalan	Hoechst	N-methyltaurino-ethylsulphone	1970

The dyebath is prepared at 50°C with:

    4% Ammonium sulphate
    2% Albegal B (Ciba—Geigy) as levelling agent,
    0.5% Albegal FFD (anti-foam agent)
    Acetic acid, if necessary
    Glauber's salt — 10% when using less than 1% dye
                5% for 1—2% dye
                nil if dye is > 2%

The bath is circulated for 10 minutes, the pH checked and adjusted to 6.5 for pale shades, down to 4.5 for heavy shades. The dye is added, the bath run for 5 minutes and the temperature raised to 70°C at 1°C per minute. Dyeing is continued at this temperature for 20 minutes, then raised to the boil at 1°C per minute and dyeing continued for 1 hour. When on shade, the bath is cooled to 80°C, the pH raised to 8—8.5 by adding 2.5% ammonia and the yarn treated for 20 minutes to remove unreacted dye. The process is completed by hot and cold rinsing.

6.5.4.2 Other Dyes

Selected 1:2 metal-complex and chrome dyes may be used for shades where reactive dyes are unsuitable or uneconomical. These dyes are applied by the methods described in Sections 6.5.2 and 6.5.3. Selected sulphonated metal-complex dyes, such as the Acidol M range, (BASF), can be used with advantage.

Reactive-dyeing methods are more expensive than conventional techniques since the cost of dyes is high and the process is lengthy, as indicated in Figure

6.8. However, reactive dyes must be used for bright shades and, in addition, conventional dyes are not sufficiently fast to washing, particularly when using detergents containing perborates.

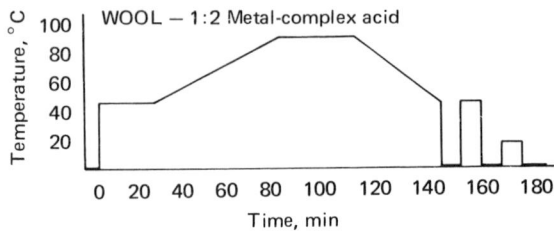

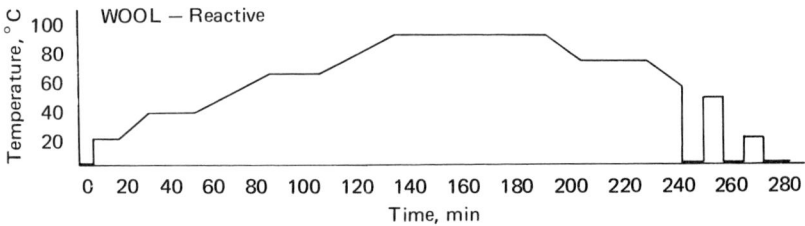

Figure 6.8 — Process profiles for dyes on wool

6.5.4.3 Dye Selection

The selection of dyes for dyeing to Superwash standards is given in Table 6.15.

TABLE 6.15

Dyes for Superwash Wool

Reactive Dyes

		C.I. Reactive
Lanasol	Yellow 4G	Yellow 39
	Orange R	Orange 68
	Red 6G	Red 84
	Red 2G	Red 116
	Red 5B	Red 66
	Blue 3R	Blue 50
	Blue 3G	Blue 69

1:2 *Metal-complex Dyes* (used for economical greens, browns and navies)

	C.I. Acid
Neutrichrome Yellow S—JRLL (as shading component only)	Yellow 121
Red S—JL (as shading component only)	Red 359
Navy S—BLL (up to 3% depth)	Blue 284
Acidol Brown M—2RL (up to 3% depth)	Brown 365

Chrome Dyes (used for navies and black)
Diamond Navy Blue RRN
Diamond Black PV

6.5.4.4 Aftertreatment of 1:2 Metal-complex Dyes

A recent development by Sandoz has been the introduction of a product, Sandopur SW, to improve the fastness of 1:2 metal-complex dyes, particularly to the IWS TM 193 washing test for Superwash wool. This product is applied as an aftertreatment in a fresh bath for 20 minutes at $50^{\circ}C$ using:

> 10% Sandopur SW

Many of the metal-complex dyes listed in Table 6.10 are improved in wet fastness by ½ to 1 grade by this aftertreatment, making them suitable for the production of a wider range of shades fast to Superwash, in preference to the more expensive reactive-dyeing method.

6.5.5 Flameproof finishes

Wool yarns for furnishing and contract-carpet uses, especially in aircraft, are given a flameproof finish, using one of the Zirpro processes, under licence from IWS. Low smoke-emission versions of the treatment are also available; with these, chrome dyes must not be used.

These treatments are readily applied as part of the package-dyeing process. The yarn is dyed with acid milling or 1:2 metal-complex dyes as described in Section 6.5.2 and then treated in a fresh bath. The acid milling and metal-complex dyes listed in Table 6.10. will withstand the process, showing no serious shade changes, while the resultant treated yarn is fast to all the agencies at the level required for contract furnishing end uses.

6.5.6 Whites

Adequate whites can be obtained by package-processing methods, using the following technique, based on bleaching with hydrogen peroxide. The degree of whiteness obtained is dependent on the base colour of the yarn, but the following procedure is typical. Treatment is carried out for 2 to 4 hours at a maximum of $50^{\circ}C$ at pH 9 to 9.5 with:

> 2 g/l tetrasodium pyrophosphate,
> 1 g/l EDTA
> 14 g/l hydrogen peroxide 35% (130 vol.).

6.5.7 Levelling of faulty dyeings

It is necessary to take great care when dyeing wool, since the correction of unlevel dyeings is difficult and wool is not resistant to lengthy and abrasive processes. Dyeings of reactive dyes cannot be satisfactorily stripped and probably the best recourse is to re-dye heavier shades or black. Acid and 1:2 metal-complex dyeings can be improved by treating the dyeing in a blank dyebath with an appropriate levelling agent. Stripping, using either sodium hydrosulphite or formic acid plus Formosul, is not satisfactory for package processing since an unlevel strip is usually obtained and thus any subsequent re-dyeing would also be unlevel.

6.5.8 Application of shrink-resist processes

The usual method of conferring shrink resistance is to treat wool slubbing continuously or to treat wool garments using batchwise techniques. The best known process is probably that based on mild acid chlorination followed by the application of Hercosett-57 (Hercules) resin. Although the ability to shrink-resist wool yarn in package form is desirable on the grounds of quicker delivery, reduced stock holding, and the possibility of leaving decisions on processing route until orders are received, the above process is not suitable.

Processes have been developed which are judged to give satisfactory results on packages in terms of the level of shrink resistance obtained and the handle of the goods produced from the yarn. One such process depends on treating the yarn by a one-bath process, firstly with Basolan DC (BASF), which is a product based on dichloroisocyanuric acid, then adding a resin, namely Basolan SW (BASF). The rate of the chlorination reaction is sensitive to pH, thus accurate control of pH is essential. The process is outlined below.

The material is treated with wetting agent and acetic acid to give the pH required:

> undyed yarns: pH 5.5
> dyed yarns or yarns to be bleached: 4.5 to 5

3% Basolan DC is added and treatment carried out for 45 minutes after which sodium bisulphite is added as an anti-chlor and treatment continued for a further 10 minutes. 1.5% Basolan SW, dissolved in water containing 3% sulphuric acid, is added to the bath and treatment continued for 30 minutes. The entire process is carried out cold and is followed by rinsing. During treatment, the liquor circulation sequence should be:

> 1 minute in the 'in' to 'out' direction
> and
> 5 minutes in the 'out' to 'in' direction

If required, the handle of the goods can be adjusted by adding 1 to 3% of Basosoft BPA (BASF) to the last rinse and treating for 15 minutes at 40°C. Rapid-drying techniques are recommended, at a temperature not exceeding 80°C.

Other similar processes which have been developed for package application include Lankrolan SHR3 (Diamond Shamrock).

6.5.9 Wool yarns in hank form

Wool yarns, especially hand-knitting and carpet yarns, are dyed in hank with acid-levelling dyes, the following trichromatic combination being suitable:

C.I. Acid Yellow 29
C.I. Acid Red 57 and
C.I. Acid Blue 72

The dyebath is prepared at 40 to 50°C with:

3% Formic (85%) or Sulphuric acid (96%)
10% Sodium sulphate (Anhydrous)

The scoured yarn is entered and the temperature raised to 98 to 100°C at a rate of 1 to 1.5°C per minute. Dyeing is continued at this temperature for 30 to 60 minutes.

Acid milling, 1:2 metal-complex, chrome or reactive dyes can also be used, but great care is required with these dyes, especially reactive dyes, when being applied to shrink-resisted yarn. 1:1 Metal-complex dyes, such as the Neolans (Ciba—Geigy), will give level dyeings of high wet fastness when applied to wool hanks, especially when using a level-dyeing assistant which allows the amount of sulphuric acid to be reduced.

Previously unpublished data [4] showed that 1:1 metal-complex dyes applied with the maximum amount of sulphuric acid gave the least strength loss, as determined by single thread strength tests, when dyeing mohair loop yarn. These results are summarized in Table 6.16.

TABLE 6.16

Loss in Strength in Dyeing Mohair Yarn

Dyeing Method	% Loss in Strength
Scoured only	8.6
1:1 Metal-complex dye with 8% sulphuric acid (96%)	27.5
1:1 Metal-complex dye with 6% sulphuric acid (96%)	28.0
Acid Milling dye	31.0
1:2 Metal-complex dye	39.1
Chrome dye	44.9

6.6 CELLULOSIC YARNS

Cotton and viscose yarns are package dyed. Typical end uses include cotton interlock knitted fabric and sewing threads. Due to the high-fastness requirements for cellulosic fibres in general, dyeing is normally carried out using reactive dyes or vat dyes, and this means that little hank dyeing is undertaken.

The package dyeing of cellulosic fibre yarns is often carried out by dyers specializing in these yarns, such as sewing thread manufacturers, since there are a number of factors associated with the processing of the yarn which makes the product difficult for a mixed-product package dyehouse to handle. These can be stated briefly as follows:

(a) Fine-count yarns are normally involved and, while this does not in itself affect dyeing production, winding production is reduced in the plant normally handling heavier-count yarns. In addition, more specialized winding machinery may be required.

(b) Dyeing times are generally longer than those with other fibres being handled.
     Vacuum extraction on dyeing machines is beneficial, especially for vat dyes.
(c) The application of the dyes requires large amounts of chemicals to be added
     portionwise, so that more labour and additional dispense tanks per machine
     may be required.
(d) Drying and conditioning are slow processes and therefore expensive. In
     addition, careful yarn conditioning is necessary, especially for knitting yarns.

6.6.1 Reactive dyes

Although oil-free yarns are normally supplied for dyeing, scouring is required to
improve wettability. This can be carried out by treating with:

> 1 g/l Anionic surface active agent, such as Levapon TH (Bayer)
> 1 g/l Soda ash

for 30 minutes at the boil. The bath is cooled to 90°C and dropped, the yarn
given a rinse at 40°C for 10 minutes, followed by a cold rinse for 10 minutes.
The yarn is lifted from the machine and the chemicals may be added manually
with the machine half-filled, because of the large quantity involved. Typical
amounts are:

> 50 g/l Salt
> 2 g/l Soda ash

The yarn is replaced and the liquor level in the machine raised to the working
level with cold water, the machine run for 5 minutes and the temperature raised
to 25°C. Reactive dyes are dissolved at temperatures not exceeding 40°C before
adding to the dyebath.

Highly reactive dyes are applied at relatively low temperature as follows. The
dye is added, and the machine run for 20 minutes at 25°C before the temperature
is raised to 40°C at 0.5°C per minute. The machine is run for 10 minutes at
40°C; soda ash, as dictated by shade, is added in three portions to the bath at
twenty-minute intervals, these amounts being, respectively, 2, 3 and 4 times the
amount added at the start, the initial amount being one tenth of the total
required.

After the final addition of soda ash, the machine is run for a further 60
minutes at 40°C and at this stage a sample can be taken and washed off for
shade assessment. When on-shade, the yarn is given the following extensive
washing-off treatment:

> Cold rinse at 20°C for 10 minutes
> Hot rinse at 60°C for 15 minutes
> Hot rinse at 70°C for 15 minutes
> Soap at the boil for 20 minutes with 1 g/l Levapon TH
> Hot rinse at 100°C for 20 minutes, twice,
> check liquor for loose colour.

A soft finish or lubricant is applied in a fresh bath.

For applying dyes of high substantivity and medium reactivity, such as the Procion HE (ICI) dyes, the following method is typical. The yarn is loaded into the machine and the liquor is circulated, the pH being adjusted to below 7 with acetic acid. The temperature is raised to 50°C and the pre-dissolved dye is added. After 15 minutes, the first portion of common salt (2.5–5 g/l) is added and after a further 25 minutes the second portion (10 – 20 g/l) is added. The temperature is then raised to 80–85°C at a rate of 1°C/minute and the remainder of the salt (17.5–65 g/l) is added. Dyeing is continued for 45 minutes at this temperature and soda ash (10 – 20 g/l) is added slowly and dyeing continued for a further 45–60 minutes. When the yarn is on-shade, the bath is dropped and processing completed by two cold rinses, soaping, a warm rinse, a cold rinse and application of finish.

6.6.2 Vat dyes

Excellent results are obtained using the Indanthren (BASF) dyes, which in general exhaust very rapidly and give a good colour yield. The dyes are classified from an application standpoint as follows:

IK dyes —   These have low substantivity for cellulose. To overcome this, they are applied at low temperature (20–25° C) with a small amount of alkali but a large addition of salt. The Indanthren range contains no IK dyes as such, but some dyes in the range can be applied by this method.

IW dyes —   These have higher substantivity. They are applied with larger amounts of caustic soda at 45–50° C.

IN dyes —   These are highly substantive. They are applied with even larger amounts of caustic soda without salt, at temperatures of 50–60° C.

IN special dyes
      —   They require more caustic soda than IN dyes, but are dyed in the same temperature range without salt.

A range of dyes which will cover a wide gamut of shades and which can all be applied by the method suitable for IW dyes is listed in Table 6.17. The amounts of chemicals required, based on a liquor ratio of 10:1, for the various application classes together with the dyeing temperatures are given in Table 6.18. In package dyeing, improved levelness can be obtained by dyeing at 80°C.

Air must be removed from the packages before dyeing is commenced, since entrapped air bubbles can cause undyed spots. A non-foaming wetting agent such as Leophen M (BASF), is useful; air can also be displaced by circulating hot water through the packages from the inside to the outside. Dyeing is usually carried out using two-way flow, with flow reversal every 3 minutes in the early stages of dyeing. Reversal may be made at longer intervals, 4 to 6 minutes, as dyeing proceeds.

Vat dyes can be applied in enclosed machines at temperatures from 25 to 115°C. Rongal HT (BASF) should be used as reducing agent, but better levelling and penetration are obtained at the elevated temperatures, while dyeing at 110

TABLE 6.17

Selection of Vat Dyes (IW Method)

C.I. Generic Name
C.I. Vat
      Yellow 46
      Orange 26
      Red 10
      Red 21
      Blue 30
      Blue 16
      Green 1
      Green 13
      Green 3
      Green 33
      Brown 55
      Black 31

TABLE 6.18

Amounts of Caustic Soda and Sodium Hydrosulphite Required for the Various Application Classes of Vat Dyes

Dye Class	Depth of dyeing (%)	Caustic Soda 38° Bé (ml/l)	Sodium Hydrosulphite (g/l)	Sodium Sulphate Anhydrous (g/l)	Dyeing Temp. (°C)
I K	0.1—1.0	6—7	2.0—2.5	7.5—10	
	1—3	7—9	2.5—3.5	10—15	20—25
	3—5	9—12	3.5—5.5	15—20	
I W	0.1—1.0	7—9	2—3	5—10	
	1—3	9—12	3—5	10—15	40—50
	3—5	12—15	5—7	15—20	
I N	0.1—1.0	15—17	3—4		
	1—3	17—22	4—6		50—60
	3—5	22—26	6—8		
I N Special	0.1—1.0	22—25	3—4		
	1—3	25—32	4—6		50—60
	3—5	32—38	6—8		

Based on a LR of 10:1

The amounts of caustic soda and hydrosulphite for preparing the stock vats are included.

to 115°C in the presence of agents such as Dekol S (BASF) will give a brightening effect which will allow pre-bleaching to be omitted in many cases. Three basic processes are used in package dyeing:

(a)   *the leuco process,* in which dyeing is commenced in the completely vatted dye solution.
(b)   *the semi-pigmentation process,* in which unvatted dye is distributed through the yarn which is then vatted as the temperature is increased,
(c)   *the pre-pigmentation process,* in which the dye is dispersed throughout the yarn followed by vatting and fixation.

It is advantageous to have a preparation tank of the same size as the dyeing machine and the feed pipes should be of wide diameter to allow for quick transfer of liquor. The leuco process is widely used and it is usual to vat in a long liquor — hence the need for large preparation tanks. The semi-pigmentation method can be considered as being intermediate between the other two processes. It has the advantage that the dye and assistants are added to the dyebath before dyeing begins, the hydrosulphite being added last to prolong the distribution of unreduced dye through the material. The semi-pigmentation method eliminates the time required for vatting in the leuco process, but the dyeing time is longer, due to the slow rate of heating needed. This method can be advantageous in automated dyehouses, since it avoids the necessity of having to make a number of additions of chemicals.

6.6.2.1 The 'Leuco' Reduced Dyeing Method

This is a two-stage procedure. The dye is reduced ('vatted') by suspending it in water, adding the alkali and reducing agent and heating until all the dye has been reduced and has completely dissolved. This 'stock' vat is then diluted with water to the correct volume.

In the second stage, the material is 'dyed' with the reduced ('leuco') dye. The leuco dye in the fibre is then converted into the original insoluble vat dye by treating the material in a dilute solution of an oxidizing agent. Finally, the dyed material is thoroughly 'soaped'.

Using the leuco method and IW class dyes, excellent results can be obtained with dyeing, rinsing, oxidizing, soaping and rinsing taking about 180 minutes. A typical recipe is:

> x% Indanthren dye
> 2 g/l Dekol S (BASF)
> y ml/l Caustic soda (as calculated from Table 6.18)
> 0.5 g/l Peregal P (BASF) (levelling agent)
> z g/l Sodium hydrosulphite ⎫
> a g/l Sodium sulphate   ⎬   (as calculated from Table 6.18)

The dye is 'vatted' at 50–60°C with sodium hydroxide and sodium hydrosulphite in the dispense tank, typical vatting times being 20–30 minutes. In the meantime, the yarn is treated in the 'blank' dyebath at the appropriate temperature (50–85°C). The stock vat is then added (often in portions over a period of (time) and dyeing continued at 50–85°C for 45–60 minutes. The yarn is then rinsed. It is oxidized in a dilute solution of either sodium perborate, hydrogen peroxide, sodium dichromate or ammonium persulphate for 20–30 minutes at the recommended temperature, followed by soaping in a dilute solution of a synthetic detergent (plus sodium carbonate in a few cases) for 15 minutes at the boil and then rinsed thoroughly.

With this method it is often difficult to control the rate of absorption of the leuco dye, and thus the risk of unlevelness and poor penetration is great. It is for this reason that the so-called 'pre-pigmentation' method was developed.

6.2.2.2 Pre-pigmentation Method

The dyebath is prepared with the dye dispersed in the required volume of water, to which a little wetting agent has been added, at a temperature of 20°C or lower. The yarn is entered, and treated in this bath for 10 minutes. The required amount of sodium hydroxide is added to the dyebath and treatment continued for 10 minutes. The required amount of reducing agent (Hydros) is added and a further 10-minute treatment of the yarn takes place. The temperature is raised to the recommended maximum temperature, at 1°C per minute, and dyeing continued at maximum temperature for 30—40 minutes. If this temperature is well above 50°C, towards the end of the period, cooling back to 50°C slowly increases the amount of dye absorbed, i.e. the colour yield is increased.

The process is completed by rinsing, oxidizing, soaping and application of finish.

At the start of the dyeing cycle, i.e. at room temperature, virtually all the dye is still in the unreduced, non-substantive form. As the temperature is raised the dye is slowly and progressively converted into the substantive leuco form. In consequence, absorption of the leuco dye is likely to be more uniform.

The higher the maximum dyeing temperature, and the longer dyeing is continued at that temperature, the greater is the degree of self-levelling. Unfortunately, the leuco compounds of a number of vat dyes gradually break down on prolonged contact with reducing agents under strongly alkaline conditions or at high temperatures. The result is a weak, off-shade dyeing.

The recommendations of the individual dyemaker must be followed.

A few dyes are sensitive to over-oxidation and care must be taken with them to use the recommended oxidizing agent and conditions. Thorough soaping is essential to stabilize the colour of the dyeing and to ensure maximum fastness to light, bleaching, rubbing and severe wet treatments generally.

6.6.2.3 The Semi-pigmentation Method

This process utilises the fact that low temperatures reduce the rate of vatting of the dyes. The dyebath is prepared at 15—20°C with the dyes and chemicals and dyeing is commenced immediately at this temperature. Unvatted pigment is distributed throughout the yarn and as vatting begins, the leuco compound penetrates into the yarn. As the temperature is raised, vatting takes place more rapidly. An advantage of this process is that all the dyes and chemicals are added at one time which can be useful in automated dyehouses. This method saves the time required for vatting in the leuco process but the dyeing time can be longer due to the slower rate of temperature rise. The semi-pigmentation process gives better levelness and penetration than the leuco process and this is an important point for tightly twisted yarns. As soon as vatting is complete, the conditions are the same as for the leuco process, with a higher dyeing temperature promoting more level dyeing. The rubbing fastness by this method is slightly inferior, so that it is mainly used for pale to medium (up to 3%) depths of shade.

6.6.3 Application of finish

Soft finish is applied in a fresh bath after dyeing, at 50°C for 20 minutes, an example being:

> 3% Sapamine KAR (CGY)
> 0.25 g/l Acetic acid (80%)

Alternatively, a wax-type emulsion can be applied at a 2% level, starting at 60°C and cooling to 40°C over 15 minutes.

6.7 DYEING OF BLENDED YARNS

The dyeing of blends has been discussed extensively by Shore [6]. Consequently, in this section, only those blends which are commonly encountered in yarn dyeing will be covered. The methods used are essentially the same as those for hanks and packages of yarn composed of one fibre. Much wool—nylon yarn is dyed in hank, especially for carpets, and these yarns are dyed using acid dyes which give solid shades on the mixture.

Acrylic — wool and acrylic—nylon blends are used for hand knitting. These can be hank dyed with advantage using acid dyes for the wool, or nylon, and Maxilon M dyes for the acrylic portion.

Although certain blends, for example, wool—nylon, are required to be dyed to solid shades, with many blends one fibre is reserved. Often the intention is to obtain a pleasing "mohair"-type look as has been mentioned earlier, but also because dyeing certain blends to solid shades is expensive. This can perhaps be justified if the solid-dyed blend yarn is to be used for the production of a stripe effect in woven or knitted fabrics or for a variation in the warp or weft direction in woven cloths. However, solid-dyed fabrics are perhaps best produced by dyeing at the fabric stage.

When dyeing contrast effects the dyes chosen for one fibre should give minimum staining of the other fibre, because of shading problems and because this stain is invariably of lower fastness, particularly to light.

Severe staining must be removed before cross-dyeing the other component. The two-stage process, with intermediate clearing and rinsing, which is necessary, is an expensive operation. In addition, rinsing processes are not highly effective in package machines.

6.7.1 Acrylic blends

6.7.1.1 Blends in which the Acrylic Portion Only is Dyed

With acrylic—wool and acrylic—nylon blends, frequently in 80:20 proportions, and acrylic—cellulosic blends, often only the acrylic component is dyed. This is partly due to the excessive cost which would be incurred using the package-dyeing route to obtain solid shades and partly because a "mohair"-type look can be obtained, especially when wool is present, by dyeing the acrylic portion only.

The dyeing of acrylic yarns has been discussed in Section 6.2.6, and a dye selection to give minimum cross-staining is given in Table 6.5. Precautions to be taken during dyeing, to capitalize on the minimum cross-stain effect, have also been discussed.

6.7.1.2 Acrylic—Wool Blends, Dyed Solid

A highly-reproducible package-dyeing technique, principally for machine-knitting yarns, has been developed by Ciba—Geigy, using Maxilon M migrating basic dyes for the acrylic portion and Lanasol reactive dyes for the wool.

The Maxilon M—Lanasol method is an expensive technique when producing heavy shades. These shades can be dyed more economically using a two-bath technique in which the basic dyes are applied first, followed by the wool dyes in a fresh bath. Basic dyes that give minimum stain on the wool are chosen according to Table 6.5. Staining on the wool component can be removed before applying the wool dyes by treating for 30 minutes at 50°C with:

> 1 g/l Hydrogen peroxide (100 vol.)
> 2 g/l Tetrasodium pyrophosphate

followed by rinsing.

The yarn is loaded into the machine and the bath is prepared at 50°C with:

> 3% Ammonium sulphate
> 5% Glauber's salt (Anhydrous)
> 0.5% Albegal A (CGY)
> 0.5% Albegal B (CGY) and
> Acetic acid to give pH 4 to 6 (lower pH for the heavier depth)

The bath is circulated for 5 minutes and the Lanasol dyes are added. The bath is run for a further 5 minutes and the temperature raised to 100°C at a rate of 1°C per minute. After 15 minutes at 100°C, the pH is adjusted to 4—5 and the Maxilon M dyes added, together with Tinegal MR if the total amount of Maxilon dye is less than 0.3%. (Dye + Tinegal MR = 0.3%.) Dyeing is continued for a further 45—60 minutes at 100°C.

For heavy shades, the bath is cooled to 80°C, the pH adjusted to 8.5 with ammonia and treatment continued for 15 minutes to remove unreacted dye. If additions of Lanasol dyes are to be made, the bath is cooled to 60°C, but the Maxilon M dyes can be added at the boil with Tinegal MR as calculated above.

A dye selection is given in Table 6.19.

TABLE 6.19

Lanasol and Maxilon M Dyes

Lanasol	Maxilon M
Yellow 4G	Yellow M 4G L
Orange R	Yellow M 3R L
Red 6G	Red M 4G L
Red 2G	Red M R L
Red 5B	Blue M 2G
Blue 3R	
Blue 3G	

6.7.1.3 Acrylic—Nylon Blends

Acrylic—nylon yarns are dyed, usually to solid shades, for both carpet and knitting end uses. In the latter category, many fancy yarns are included, often of the bouclé or poodle type. Basic dyes are used for the acrylic portion and acid milling or 1:2 metal-complex dyes for the nylon.

For pale-to-medium shades, a one-bath, two-stage method is used. The bath is prepared at 50°C with acetic acid to give a pH of 4.5, the calculated amount of retarder, based on the weight of acrylic fibre only, the nylon dyes and 1% Avolan IWF (Bayer). The temperature is raised to 85°C at 1°C per minute, the basic dyes added, the temperature raised to 100°C at 0.25°C per minute and dyeing continued for 30 minutes.

For full shades, the bath is prepared at 70°C with acetic acid to give a pH of 4.5, 1% Avolan IWF (Bayer), retarder calculated as above, and the basic dyes. The temperature is raised rapidly to 85°C, then from 85 to 95°C at 0.25°C per minute and dyeing continued at this temperature. The slow RAMP may be continued to 100°C for exhaustion. The bath is then cooled to 50°C, the nylon dyes added, the temperature raised to 100°C at 1°C per minute and dyeing continued at this temperature until satisfactory exhaustion is achieved. The yarn is cooled and rinsed to complete the process.

Suitable dyes for the acrylic component are listed in Table 6.5, and for the nylon in Table 6.10.

The Alcosist CTL method (see Section 6.2.5) is useful for dyeing this blend.

Alcosist CTL is an excellent anti-precipitant, and can be used with Alcosist PL or Alcosist PN flake (Allied Colloids) to dye acrylic—nylon blends. Because Alcosist CTL completely reserves the acrylic fibre up to the boil, it is possible to dye the blended yarn as 100% nylon.

Great care should be taken when preparing the dyebath, and it is essential that the dyes and chemicals are added in the following sequence:

1. Acid dyes
2. Chemicals and auxiliaries
3. Basic dyes

The amount of Alcosist CTL required depends on the type of yarn and depth of shade, exactly as for the 100% acrylic yarn, and should be calculated on the weight of acrylic fibre present. The amount of Alcosist PL and of Alcosist PN flake required depend on the depth of shade and composition of the blend, most product being required for heavy shades and 50:50 blends.

A typical dye recipe is:

> x% Acid dyes
> y% Alcosist CTL (according to the calculation)
> 2—4% Alcosist PL
> or   0.25 — 1 g/l Alcosist PN flake
> z% Basic dyes
> Acid to pH 4.5—5.0

The dyebath should be prepared at 40°C and the temperature raised to the boil over 40—60 minutes; boiling is continued for 30—60 minutes according to depth of shade.

6.7.1.4 Acrylic—Modacrylic Blends

Modacrylic fibres are blended with acrylic fibres to reduce the fire hazard for end uses such as carpets and furnishings; this blending is mandatory for floor-coverings in North America. A common practice is to include 40% of modacrylic fibre such as Teklan, Kanekalon, etc. The bath is prepared with:

> 10% Glauber's salt (Anhydrous)
> 2% Acetic acid (80%)
> Retarder, calculated on the weight of acrylic fibre
>   (60% of the total in the above example.)

The temperature is raised to 90°C at 0.25°C per minute and run for 30 minutes. The bath is then cooled to 50°C, before the yarn is removed from the machine.

The number of dyes which meet fastness and solid-dyeing requirements is limited. The following are those which have commonly been used successfully:

> C.I. Basic Yellow 28
> C.I. Basic Red 46
> C.I. Basic Blue 41

6.7.1.5 Acrylic—Cellulose Triacetate

This blend is used mainly for fancy yarns for machine knitting. Before dyeing is begun, the machine must be boiled out in presence of some of the carrier to be used for the triacetate. Cationic retarders must not be used.

Pale shades are dyed by a one-bath, two-stage process. The bath is prepared at 40°C with:

> 0.5% Acetic acid (80%)
> 1% Sunaptol LT [ADC] (dispersing agent)
> 1 g/l Optinol TR [YCL] (carrier)
> and the Disperse dyes

The temperature of the bath is raised to 80°C at 0.5°C per minute and the basic dyes added. The temperature is then raised to 98°C at 0.25°C per minute and dyeing continued at 98°C for 30 minutes.

For dark shades, the bath is prepared at 60°C with:

> the Basic dyes
> 1% Sunaptol LT
> Acetic acid to give pH 4.5

The temperature of the bath is raised to 98°C at 0.5°C per minute and dyeing continued at this temperature for 30 minutes. The bath is then cooled to 80°C, and the disperse dyes and 1 g/l Optinol TR are added. The temperature is again raised to 98°C at 0.5°C per minute and dyeing continued for 30 minutes.

The dyed yarn is rinsed in cold water, cleared with 0.5 ml/l sodium hypochlorite for 20 minutes at 40°C and given an anti-chlor with 0.5 g/l sodium metabisulphite plus 0.5 g/l sodium bicarbonate for 20 minutes at 50°C. A cold rinse completes the process.

For whites, the bath is prepared with:

> 0.5% Acetic acid (80%)
> 1 g/l Optinol TR (Y.C.L.)
> 1% Sunaptol LT (Alliance)
> x% Blankophor DC BR (Bayer) and
> y% Fluolite XMF (ICI) both according to shade

The temperature is raised to 98°C at 0.5°C per minute and dyeing carried out for 30 minutes.

In all cases, a soft finish is applied in a fresh bath, using 2% Alcamine PF (Allied Colloids) and acetic acid, at pH 5.5 for 20 minutes at 85°C.

6.7.2 Polyester blends

6.7.2.1 Polyester—Cellulosic Blends

In yarn form, these are generally processed by the methods described earlier for polyester yarns leaving the cellulosic component undyed. Such yarns can be dyed to solid shades with Cottestren (BASF) dyes. These are mixtures of selected Indanthren (BASF) vat dyes for the cellulosic component and selected Palanil (BASF) disperse dyes for the polyester portion. High-temperature dyeing methods are used in which the disperse dye is first applied to the polyester followed by the fixation of the vat dye. Typically, dyeing is carried out using a liquor ratio of 10:1, the dyebath being prepared at 70°C with the Cottestren dyes, dispersing agent and acetic acid to give a pH of 4.5 to 5. The temperature is raised to 130°C at 1°C per minute and dyeing continued at that temperature for 30 to 60 minutes, depending on depth of shade.

During the high-temperature dyeing stage, the disperse dye is absorbed by the polyester component and the cellulose portion is evenly pigmented with the vat dye. The bath is then cooled to 80°C; caustic soda, sodium hydrosulphite and 0.5 to 1 g/l Peregal P (BASF) are added to the bath in that order. Dyeing is carried out for 15 minutes at 80°C with a further 15 minutes at 50 to 60°C for heavy shades.

The amounts of chemicals required for a liquor ratio of 10:1 are given in Table 6.20.

TABLE 6.20

Concentrations of Chemicals required for Cottestren Dyes

Dye (%)	Caustic Soda 38° Bé (ml/l)	Sodium Hydrosulphite (g/l)
up to 2%	10—12	3—4
2—5%	14—16	4—5
5—10%	16—20	5—7
Over 10% and black	25—30	8—9

With certain Indanthren dyes which are susceptible to over-reduction, an amount of sodium nitrite, equal to 15% of the amount of hydrosulphite used, should be added. With certain dyes, the addition of 10 to 15 g/l sodium sulphate anhydrous will increase the colour yield. Following dyeing, the yarn is rinsed, oxidized and soaped in the manner outlined earlier.

6.7.2.2 Polyester—Wool Blends

Polyester—wool blends, often in the proportions 55:45, are widely used, especially for suitings. These yarns can be dyed with disperse dyes for the polyester component and acid milling or metal-complex dyes for the wool. Dyeing is normally carried out at either 105° or 120°C, although the latter method requires the addition of a protecting agent to the dyebath e.g formaldehyde solution.

The selection of disperse dyes is carried out on the basis of:
- — minimum staining of the wool
- — availability of a carrier which will give good exhaustion, not increase the disperse dye stain on the wool and not reduce the light fastness
- — high light fastness
- — minimum interaction with the wool dyes.

There are several advantages in using premixed dyes for dyeing this blend, particularly if the production is not large. These include:

- good shade solidity
- reduced stock holding
- only three dyes (not six) are needed in ternary mixtures
- most mixtures will be satisfactory over a range of blend proportions.

A disadvantage is that premixed dyes are more expensive than purchasing separate dyes for the two components.

The method of application of such mixtures is as follows. The bath is prepared at $50°C$ with:

> 3% Ammonium sulphate
> Formic acid to give pH of 5.5 to 6.0
> 1.5 to 4 g/l Dilatin TCR (Sandoz), depending on depth of shade.

The temperature of the bath is raised to $105°C$ at $1.5°C$ per minute and dyeing continued for 60–100 minutes at that temperature to achieve exhaustion. The yarn is rinsed well and scoured for 20 minutes at $70°C$ with:

> 1 g/l Sufatol LS 3 (Standard Chemicals) and
> 0.5% Acetic acid

Rinsing completes the process. Suitable dyes for the dyeings normally required can be obtained from ranges such as:

> Forosyn (S)
> Lanastren (BASF)
> Resolamine (Bayer)
> Teralan (CGY)

while the range of shades normally required, for example, for the production of woven men's suitings can be obtained using a small range of dyes such as:

> Forosyn Yellow HSG
> Red HSN
> Navy HSN
> Brown HS
> Grey HS.

6.7.3 Blends with nylon

6.7.3.1 Differential-dyeing Nylon

These yarns have been discussed in Section 6.4.7.

6.7.3.2 Vincel (Courtaulds)–Nylon

This blend has found some popularity in the manufacture of crepe-type fancy yarns. Normally, the nylon portion only is dyed owing to the high cost of a double dyeing process. In this case, the nylon component is dyed with acid milling or 1:2 metal-complex dyes, according to the methods given in Section 6.4. An alternative method is to pretreat the yarn at $50°C$ for 15 minutes with 4%

Lyogen P(S) and 0.5% acetic acid (80%), then add the dye. The temperature is raised to 100°C at 1°C per minute and dyeing continued for 30 minutes. The process is completed with a cold rinse.

If both fibre components are to be dyed, the Vincel is dyed with reactive dyes and then the nylon dyed, using a two-bath process.

Bleaching may be required before dyeing to obtain good quality pastel colours, or white on the undyed portion. The following procedure is typical, using a 15:1 liquor-to-goods ratio. The yarn is treated for 30 minutes at 60°C with:

> 2 g/l Sodium chlorite liquid
> 1 g/l Tannex special (Tanatex)
> Acetic acid, to give a pH of 3.8

The yarn is rinsed and given a further treatment for 20 minutes at 60°C with:

> 2 g/l Sodium bisulphite
> 2 g/l Sodium bicarbonate

followed by rinsing.

6.7.4 Blends of wool and nylon

Traditionally, up to 10% of nylon has been blended with wool in weaving or knitting yarns to improve yarn strength. More widely used is the 80:20 blend of wool—nylon for carpet yarns, the nylon component improving the wear resistance of the resultant carpet.

These yarns are dyed with acid milling and 1:2 metal-complex dyes, usually in the presence of a nylon-blocking agent, to obtain consistently good solidity and excellent fastness. Suitable dyes are listed in Table 6.10.

A guide to the quantity of blocking agent required is indicated in Table 6.21, but individual dyes and blends may require specific amounts, particularly for different types of nylon.

TABLE 6.21

Nylon Blocking Agent Requirements

	Depth of Shade (%)	Erional RF (CGY) (%)
Acid Milling	0—1	1—2
	1—2	0.5—1.5
	above 2	0—1
1:2 Metal-complex	0—1	2—3
	1—2	1.5—2.5
	above 2	0.5—1.5

Conventional 1:2 metal-complex dyes require more blocking agent than the more recently developed sulphonated (S) brands. The dyebath is prepared at 40°C with 1% acetic acid and e.g. Erional RF (Ciba—Geigy) as calculated from Table 6.21. The temperature is raised to 100°C at 1°C per minute and dyeing continued for 30 minutes.

REFERENCES

1. Mackin, *J.S.D.C.*, **91** (1975) 75;
   Mackin and Purves, *ibid.*, **96** (1980) 177.
2. Biedermann, *Rev. Prog. Coloration*, **10** (1979) 1.
3. Resolin S Process, *Bayer Publication*, Sp. 456.
4. ICI, *Technical Information Note* D 1389.
5. Blackburn and Gallagher, *J.S.D.C.*, **96** (1980) 237.
6. Shore, in *'The Dyeing of Synthetic-polymer and Acetate Fibres'* ed. D. M. Nunn, (Bradford: Dyers Company Publications Trust, 1979) p. 411 *et seq.*
7. Burnett and Park, unpublished work (1959).
8. Heane, Hill, Park and Shore, *J.S.D.C.*, **95**, (1979), 125;
   Park and Shore *J.S.D.C.*, **97** (1981), 223.

CHAPTER 7

Back winding

7.1 PACKAGE YARN

With parallel-sided packages, following dyeing and drying, it is conventional practice to re-wind the yarn on to cones for delivery. The inclusion of a back-winding operation in the processing route is beneficial because it is a secondary quality inspection point, yarn can be mechanically cleared and large knots removed, etc., and lubricants can be applied to obtain the correct frictional properties for subsequent processing.

7.1.1 Staple yarns

For machine-knitting and weaving yarns, waxes are generally used for staple yarns. While a certain minimum quantity of lubricant is required for optimum results, above this level the frictional resistance again increases and perform-ance deteriorates. At a load of 10–20g on the wax disc, paraffin waxes (m.p. 60–70°C) give the best lubrication and minimum fly. Softeners can adversely affect lubrication. Yarns for carpets and hand knitting are not waxed.

A thread-up of a typical winding machine for back winding staple yarns is shown in Figure 7.1.

Many automatic winding machines are available, often equipped with auto-matic doffing and knotting, and either manual or electronic clearers. In sophisti-cated machines, such as those manufactured by Savio, centralized control systems are available to ensure uniform operation of all spindles by regulating yarn tension, waxing pressure, package counter-weighting and speed changes. Automatic machines are perhaps best suited for fine-count yarns where a high allocation of spindles per operative is possible, especially when magazine-type creeling devices are used.

Manual winding machines may be adequate for many yarn-dyeing operations, especially if coarser-count yarns are being handled. Both types of machine are capable of preparing cones or parallel-sided packages, giving winding speeds of 800–1000 metres per minute, but there are considerable differences in cost. Automatic machines cost approximately £1000–1400 per winding position, whereas manual machines cost £250–£500 per winding position. Fadis have an interesting machine which, with a minor modification, will wind both staple and continuous filament yarns, which is important when versatility is required.

If a replacement programme is envisaged, careful costings must be carried

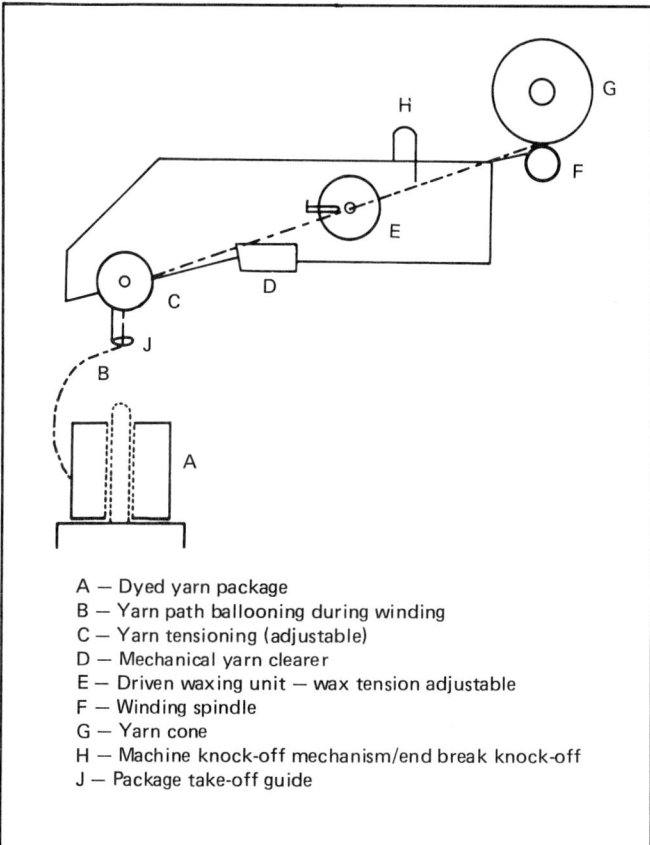

A — Dyed yarn package
B — Yarn path ballooning during winding
C — Yarn tensioning (adjustable)
D — Mechanical yarn clearer
E — Driven waxing unit — wax tension adjustable
F — Winding spindle
G — Yarn cone
H — Machine knock-off mechanism/end break knock-off
J — Package take-off guide

Figure 7.1 — Cone winding machine

out with regard to machine cost, operating cost as influenced by manning levels and energy use, maintenance requirements, the space required, and the pay-back period for the capital invested. It would also appear that with hosiery yarns there is a movement towards the use of $5°$ 57′ cones, since these give better efficiencies in machine knitting and a more stable cone build compared with the traditional $9°$ 15′ cone [1]. Cone traverse for staple yarns is usually 150–210 mm.

For winding packages of carpet yarn, either for dyeing, or cones for carpet manufacture, it would be difficult to better the Gilbos GF 10R winder, and a six-head machine will produce approximately 7 tonnes in 40 hours.

A balanced plant is also required, so that back-winding capacity is in line with the preparation capacity and the amount of yarn from the dyehouse which is to be rewound. Typical production rates are as follows: a Hacoba/Fadis relaxation machine will produce 2.04 kg per spindle hour when running at 670 metres per minute at an efficiency of 85% on a 2/30 worsted count yarn. This is equivalent to 3900 kg from a 16-end unit running for 120 hours. On the same yarn, a modern manual rewinding machine will produce 2.44 kg per spindle hour when running at 800 metres per minute at 85% efficiency. This is equivalent to 4685 kg from a 48-end unit running for 40 hours per week.

7.1.2 Continuous filament yarns

These yarns are usually rewound on to "pineapple" cones, conicity 3° 30' and traverse 300—360 mm on a machine with a thread-up as shown in Figure 7.2.

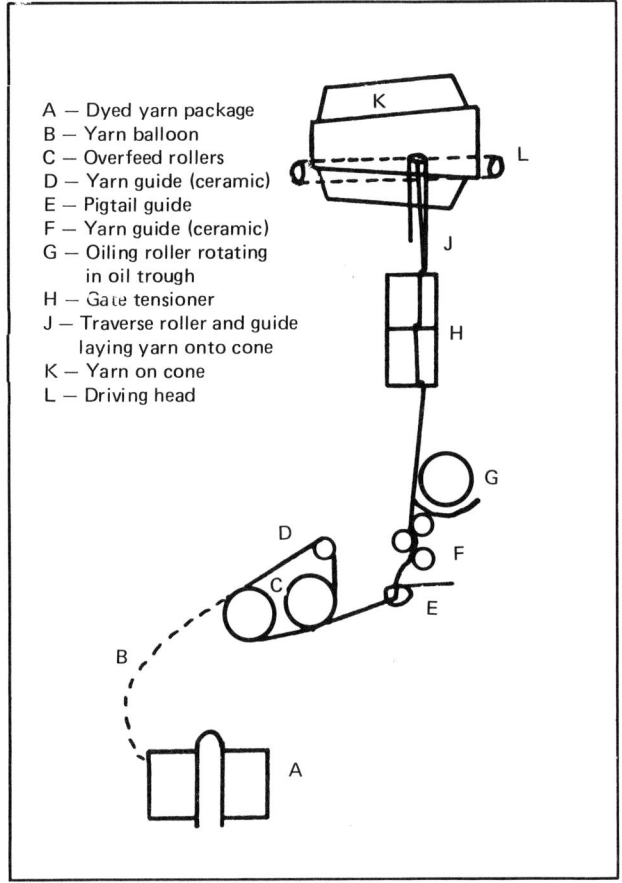

A — Dyed yarn package
B — Yarn balloon
C — Overfeed rollers
D — Yarn guide (ceramic)
E — Pigtail guide
F — Yarn guide (ceramic)
G — Oiling roller rotating
    in oil trough
H — Gate tensioner
J — Traverse roller and guide
    laying yarn onto cone
K — Yarn on cone
L — Driving head

Figure 7.2. — Thread-up of machine for continuous filament yarns

Lubricating oils are generally used for continuous filament yarns, and some softeners are effective lubricants. In selecting lubricating oils, cost, scourability, colour, resistance to oxidation, viscosity, non-splashing and non-rusting properties (from an environmental standpoint and when running a mixed winding plant) and their effect on dye fastness must be considered. Up to 4% of lubricant is usually applied to knitting yarns, but as little as 1% for weaving yarns.

7.1.3 Winding machine manufacturers

Suitable winding machines for both staple and continuous filament yarns can be obtained from a number of manufacturers including those listed in Table 7.1.

TABLE 7.1

Winding Machine Manufacturers

Company	Address
Savio	Arsizio, Italy
Talleres Rof	Sabadell, Barcelona, Spain
Scharer	Zurich, Switzerland
Motocono	Tarrasa, Barcelona, Spain
Mettler	Greifensle, Switzerland
Schweiter	Horgen, Switzerland
Fadis	Solbiate Arno Varese, Italy
Ott and Kolbus	Kempten, W. Germany
Corghi	Correggio, Italy
Hirshburger	Reutlingen, W. Germany
Sahm	Eschwege, W. Germany
Zerbo	Brusnengo, Italy
Gilbos	Aalst, Belgium
Schlafhokst	Munchengladbach, W. Germany

7.1.4 Elimination of winding

Winding is a time-consuming and costly operation and does not add to the intrinsic value of the yarn. Cost of winding will be discussed in Chapter 8, but the elimination of winding wherever possible is a worthwhile objective on both technical and economic grounds. Subsequent processors, such as weavers or knitters, have generally insisted on rewinding for the reasons given above regarding quality inspection, clearing and lubrication, unless a substantial reduction in the cost of the product to them could be given.

Dyeing on cone is one possible method of eliminating at least one winding process but, as mentioned in earlier chapters, this method of dyeing can give rise to technical problems and inspection, etc., is not possible since rewinding does not take place. Other savings in winding operations mentioned earlier include spinning or twisting directly on to the dyepack.

With the use of parallel-sided dyepacks and press-packing techniques or the use of the recently developed BI—KO centre, a package can be produced which is stable throughout dyeing, gives rise to no technical problems and is stable and sufficiently well presented to be used as the supply package for the next process, whether this be twisting (in the case of dyed singles yarn), knitting, weaving or tufting. With yarns that require lubrication, this can now be carried out in the dyebath as a final process, and application is more even than in waxing by disc on the winding machine. Although such application is more costly than waxing, it is worthwhile if winding is eliminated. The soft finish, if required, is applied in the usual manner during dyeing, then the lubricant is applied in a final bath at pH 6 for 20 minutes at 60°C. Products such as Supporter BKK (Rudolph & Co.) or Alcolube PKL (Allied Colloids), applied at a level of 2%, have been found to give satisfactory results as judged by frictional properties and knittability. When dyebath lubricants are applied, less soft finish is usually required to obtain a given handle.

7.2 HANK YARN

Following dyeing and drying, hank yarn is invariably rewound on to a suitable supply package for the next process or for sale. With machine-knitting and weaving yarns, this is usually on to cone, the conicity of the cone being 9° 15' or, more recently, 5° 57'. Waxes are generally applied during cone winding.

Hand-knitting yarns are often wound on to a cone or an alternative type of suitable package before being balled into sales packages. Carpet yarns are often rewound by the carpet manufacturer on to packages, such as bobbins or spools, to suit the type of loom used.

In cone winding, the hank is carefully loaded on to the swift of the machine, to avoid further entanglement and the generation of excess waste. Manual machines are normally used and winding speeds of 350 metres per minute are not generally exceeded in hank-to-cone winding. The thread-up of a typical hank-to-cone-winding machine is shown in Figure 7.3.

A number of manufacturers supply winding machines suitable for hank-to-cone winding, and many of these will also wind from package to cone, provided that the thread-up is slightly modified and the yarn speed is increased. Suitable hank-to-cone winding machines can be obtained from a number of machinery manufacturers, including those listed in Table 7.2.

TABLE 7.2
Hank-to-cone Winding Machine Manufacturers

Company	Address
Corghi	Correggio, Italy
Fadis	Solbiate Arno, Italy
Gilbos	Aalst, Belgium
Leesona	Warwick, Rhode Island, USA
Mettier	Arth, Switzerland
Motocono	Tarrasa, Barcelona, Spain
Murata	Kyoto, Japan
ROF	Sabadel, Barcelona, Spain
Savio	Pordenone, Italy

ompensator device

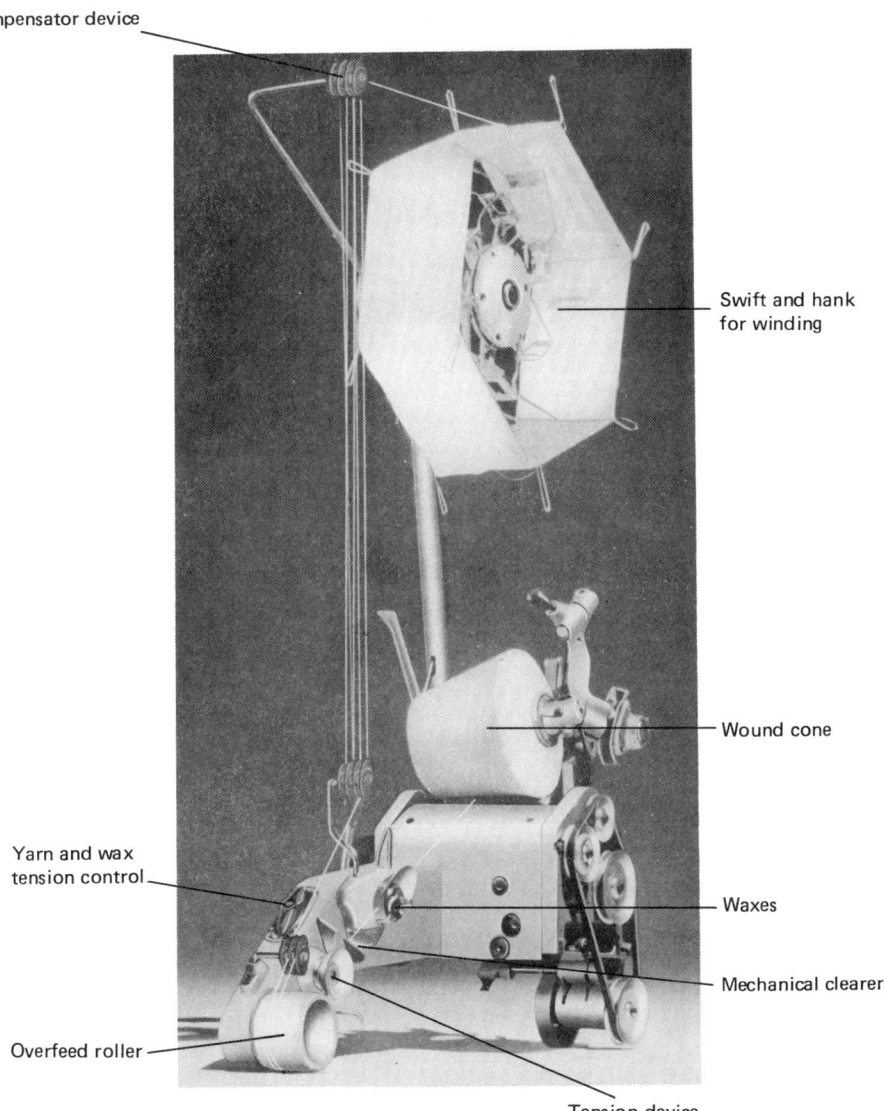

Swift and hank
for winding

Wound cone

Yarn and wax
tension control

Waxes

Mechanical clearer

Overfeed roller

Tension device

Figure 7.3 – Thread-up of hank-to-cone winding machine

REFERENCE

1. Klosges, *Textile Asia* (May 1979) p. 57.

CHAPTER 8

Costs and cost comparisons

The cost of processing for package dyeing and ancillary processing, as for any dyeing operation, can be readily ascertained by determining the cost of each individual item involved in production. The distribution of these unit costs for acrylic and wool yarns, according to the various areas of cost, is given in Table 8.1. These costs are shown as percentages of the total as well as in terms of the dye and chemical costs (x for acrylic and y for wool). This latter method of expressing cost, whilst making it less plant-specific, also makes costs less time-dependent, since all costs are almost equally effected by factors such as inflation.

TABLE 8.1

Cost Areas for Total Processing of Acrylic and Wool Yarns based on a Two-wind Operation

	Acrylic		Wool	
	Expressed in terms of:			
	Dyes & Chemicals (x)	% of Total	Dyes & Chemicals (y)	% of Total
Depreciation	$2.26 x$	30.2	$1.33 y$	27.6
Overheads	$0.77 x$	10.3	$0.45 y$	9.4
Wages & Salaries	$2.32 x$	30.8	$1.36 y$	28.3
Energy, Water, etc.	$0.5 \ x$	6.5	$0.3 \ y$	5.9
Dyes & Chemicals	$1.0 \ x$	13.4	$1.0 \ y$	20.7
Transport, Cartons, Cones	$0.66 x$	8.8	$0.4 \ y$	8.1
	$7.51 x$	100	$4.84 y$	100

$$y = 1.7 x$$

An alternative method of expressing costs is according to cost centre. This is given in Table 8.2 for a typical package-dyeing operation.

TABLE 8.2

Cost Distribution according to Cost Centre

	%
Preliminary handling and warehousing	4
Preparatory winding	15
Dyeing and drying, incl. dyes and chemicals	45
Back-winding	21
Packing, inspection, despatch, transport	15
	100

This table indicates the importance of attempting to eliminate winding operations, since double winding accounts for 36% of total costs.

If the dyehouse costs (dyeing and drying) are further examined, a breakdown, as shown in Table 8.3. is obtained for various fibre types.

TABLE 8.3

Areas of Dyehouse Cost (%)

	Acrylic	Polyester	Nylon	Wool
Services	14—17	15—21	15—17	10—12
Wages	20—22	16—18	16—18	13—14
Overheads	28—33	25—28	24—27	20—21
Dyes & Chemicals	30—40	32—45	39—44	55

8.1 EFFECT OF LEVEL OF INVESTMENT

The cost of production is influenced by the depreciation which has to be borne, and this in turn is related to the level of investment in new plant, services, etc. A distribution of costs for the installation of a new dyehouse and a partial replacement project is given in Table 8.4.

TABLE 8.4

Breakdown of Costs (Dyehouse Only)

Work	Partial Scheme (%)	Greenfield Scheme (%)
Building	26	46.5
Pipework/steam/valves	21	17.5
Dyeing machines, etc.	33	29.0
Control system	7	2.3
Electrical	13	4.7
Approx. cost	£0.6 m	£2.0 m

This level of investment and its effect on the dyeing cost of acrylic yarn is given in Table 8.5, expressed in terms of x (the dye and chemical cost.) Table 8.6 gives the total cost, including a double winding operation, for acrylic and wool yarns. These two tables also include the desired selling prices to cover a profit margin and contingencies, together with an indication of the market price obtainable.

These tables indicate that only a limited level of investment is possible for the dyeing of acrylic yarns, but that up-market products, such as wool yarns, will enable a total greenfield operation to be established and a profit margin, etc., to be achieved.

TABLE 8.5

Dyeing Cost

Level of Investment	Cost Price (p/kg)	Desired Selling Price (p/kg)
No depreciation	3.1 x	3.84 x
Reorganized with 20% new machines	3.25 x	4.1 x
All machinery new	3.4 x	4.2 x
Greenfield	3.54 x	4.4 x
Market price		4.08 x

TABLE 8.6

Cost for Total Process on Greenfield Site

	Acrylic	Wool
Cost price	7.5 x	4.84 y
Desired selling price	8.6 x	5.57 y
Market price	7.1 x	5.7 y

$$y = 1.7 x$$

8.2 COMPARISON OF COLORATION ROUTE

With synthetic fibres, a serious competitor to package dyeing in recent years has been continuous tow-dyeing. Although less flexible and less able to adjust quickly to changes in fashion shades, it gives considerable cost savings. Table 8.7 indicates the differences in cost between package dyeing and continuous tow dyeing of acrylic fibres. Most of the additional cost of package dyeing can be associated with the extra winding operations.

TABLE 8.7

Cost Comparison of Dyeing Processes for Acrylic Fibres

Dyeing Route	Cost Ratio
Continuous tow dyeing	35
Package dyeing, including double winding	
— cost only	80
plus margins and contingencies	100
Package delivered on dyepack	
— cost only	61
plus margins and contingencies	77

8.3 COMPARISON OF PROCESS ROUTE

The cost of dyed acrylic yarn on cone ready for delivery to the knitter is given in Table 8.8 in which a comparison of various spinning and coloration routes is made. The coloration processes considered include package dyeing, tow dyeing and producer-dyeing. These prices, which include the necessary margin, are compared with the market sales price which is taken as 100. As mentioned above, both continuous methods are less versatile than package dyeing, particularly for short runs of fashion shades.

TABLE 8.8

Comparison of Process Route Costs for Acrylic Yarn

	Price of Dyed Yarn on Cone
Ring spun yarn, package dyed in existing dyehouse	116
greenfield dyehouse	127
Non-ring spun yarn, packaged dyed in existing dyehouse	104
Ring spun yarn, spun directly on to dyepack and package dyed in existing dyehouse	109
Ring spun, producer dyed	95
Ring spun, continuous tow dyed	104
Market sales price	100

8.4 ELIMINATION OF WINDING

In previous sections, there have been several references to the elimination of winding as an economic and technical objective. Table 8.9 indicates the dyeing costs and the savings which can be made in the dyehouse alone by the use of parallel-sided dyepack or BI—KO in preference to cone. Much of the saving incurred is related to the larger payloads obtained by press-packing techniques which in turn influence the cost of water, effluent, energy, dye and chemicals per kilo of yarn dyed.

A further indication of the savings which can be obtained is given in Table 8.10, in which various process routes are compared. The greatest savings are obtained if the yarn can be spun directly on to the former which will also constitute the delivery package, thereby eliminating two winding operations. This technique probably has greatest potential when allied to open-end spinning, or the ability to two-for-one twist directly on to the dye package. The costings given in Table 8.10 are based on regular-spun acrylic yarn and include the cost of the fibre.

8.5 EVALUATION OF ALTERNATIVE PROCESSING ROUTES

Although it has been indicated in previous sections that package dyeing can make a process more expensive, due to the extra winding costs involved, and that it may be concluded that, in certain areas, the future viability of package

TABLE 8.9

Dyeing Cost Related to Package Type

	Cone	BI–KO	Parallel-sided Dyepack
Expressed as x, the dye and chemical cost	3.47 x	2.77 x	2.33 x
% of dyepack method	148	118	100

TABLE 8.10

Comparison of Process Route Costs for Acrylic yarn

Process Route

	A	B	C	D
	Spin (normal) Wind/supp. cone Prep. dyepack Dye and dry Rewind on to cone	Spin Wind on cone Dye and dry	Spin/dyepack Dye and dry Rewind on to cone	Spin/former to be used as final supply pack Dye and dry
Cost price of dyed yarn on cone (inc. fibre) as % of Route A	100	93	88	84
Total cost as % of spinning cost (inc. fibre)	152	141	134	127

dyeing may depend on the elimination of winding processes, it is essential to evaluate the various processing routes possible.

Although the cost of a particular route is important, other benefits of a given route must be considered and may be the over-ruling factors. These include shorter delivery times, elimination of processes, better quality in terms of physical properties, ease of later manufacturing processes, levelness (or fastness) and flexibility. The diminishing differences between prices of different types of dyeing machine, and the possible use of multi-purpose machines (e.g. with different cages) should be considered. Since it is difficult to follow fashion colours which can change rapidly, the major stock held should be in the ecru (grey) state, with dyeing being carried out as late as possible in the manufacturing cycle.

The cost of dyeing carpet yarn at various stages of the manufacturing route is shown in Table 8.11, expressed in terms of x, the cost of converting fibre to yarn.

TABLE 8.11

Comparison of Carpet Yarn Dyeing Costs

Loose stock	Hank	Package
Dyeing	Spinning on to	Spinning on to
	twisting bobbin	bobbin
Spinning up to		Package formation
twisting bobbin	Hank reeling	and dyeing
Cone winding	Dyeing	1.55 x
	Cone winding	Plus rewind
		1.64 x
		Plus large
		cone rewind
1.52 x	1.86 x	1.71 x

The above comparison of costs does not take into account any beneficial effect on cash flow of a reduction in stock which may be possible, or savings due to such factors as the elimination of waste, particularly coloured wastes, from spinning and winding processes.

8.6 OPTIMIZATION OF DYEING PROCESSES

It has been emphasized throughout that the package-dyeing process, in all its aspects, is amenable to a high degree of control, resulting in a high level of reproducibility, which, in turn, enables a high level (90 to 95%) of blind or 'no-addition' dyeings to be achieved. This will give very large cost savings when operated in conjunction with careful dye selection so that dyes are chosen, whenever possible, on cost-effective grounds. This will include:

— the use of dyes of intrinsically high fastness properties so that aftertreatments are unnecessary
— with polyester, the use of auxiliary systems to eliminate reduction clearing
— with wool, the use of conventional dyes
— the use of dyeing methods based on calculation techniques.

The effect of dyeing costs on process optimization is shown in Table 8.12.

TABLE 8.12

Effect of Process Optimization

Fibre Type	Process Details	Comparative Cost
Acrylic	Blind dye	100
	Rapid blind dye	108
	One-addition process	127
Polyester	Blind dye	111
	Rapid blind dye	119
	Blind dye plus reduction-clear	134
	One-addition	136
	One-addition plus reduction-clear	160
Nylon	Blind dye	99
	Blind dye plus syntan	128
	Blind dye plus back-tan	163
Wool	Blind dye, conventional dyes	119
	Blind dye, reactive dyes	197

These costs indicate that rapid dyeing of acrylic yarn gives an increase in cost due to the higher cost of chemicals, which is not off-set by the time saving. However, rapid dyeing of polyester is advantageous, provided that the chemical system used allows the elimination of reduction-clearing treatments.

The effect of the above changes on the total operation, including double winding is given in Table 8.13 for a mixed production of:

Acrylic	50%
Polyester	15%
Nylon	15%
Wool	20%

TABLE 8.13

Effect on Total Process Cost of Changes in Dyeing Procedure

Process	Comparative Cost
Blind dye	100
No addition (conventional dyeing)	102
Average 0.3 Additions/dyelot	110
Blind dye plus 33% redips	116
Conventional dyeing plus 0.3 additions (on average) per dyelot and 5% reprocessing	112

Conventional dyeing means that the dyeing is sampled and assessed for shade, even if no addition is necessary. Blind dyeing means that, with established, reproducible recipes, the material is not examined until it reaches the quality control department. Costings have shown that blind dyeing is more economical than conventional dyeing, provided that not more than 20% of the blind dyeings produced require to be re-dipped.

The effect of process optimisation and automatic control on plant requirements to obtain a given production cannot be overlooked. This is considered for a model dyehouse situation in Table 8.14, in which the effect on the production capacity of reducing cycle times from six hours, which would be considered by most dyehouses to be quite reasonable, to four, or even three, hours is given.

This model situation underlines the dangers of over-equipping, as well as the development of an over-capacity situation with the attendant possibility of plant imbalance in other production areas, when establishing a new dyehouse or re-equipping an existing one, if account is not taken of true cycle times.

TABLE 8.14

Model Dyehouse

Machine distribution — 4 machines
One machine each of capacity — 100, 200, 400 and 800 kg
Machine capacity per cycle — 1500 kg

Working for 120 hours per week, the dyehouse capacity is 180,000 kg/h
With a cycle time of 6 hours, actual dyeing capacity is 30 tonnes per week
"   4   "   45   "
"   3   "   60   "

Throughout this book, an attempt has been made to show that package dyeing of yarn is a high-technology operation, capable of a high level of control. This control can be used to increase productivity and reduce cost. A measure of the advances made in the technology of package dyeing can be obtained by comparing the productivity per machine-hour obtainable by existing technology in 1970 as compared to that obtainable a decade later.

In 1970, a Henriksen GRU 150 would give a payload of 250 kg, based on existing package specifications and manual loading. With conventional dyeing techniques and the necessity to make one dye addition to every third dyeing, such a machine would give a productivity of 58 kg per machine-hour.

In 1980, by using larger packages, press-packing techniques, optimized, if not rapid, dyeing techniques, and by blind dyeing, the same dyeing machine will give a productivity of 140 kg per machine hour. This represents an increase in productivity to 240% on the 1970 figure.

8.7 COMPARISONS BETWEEN PACKAGE AND HANK PROCESSING

Much has been stated in earlier sections regarding the relative merits of hank and package processing, and, in turn, this has given some insight as to the relative costs. Table 8.11 compares the costs of hank and package routes as regards the processing of carpet yarn.

Practical experience has shown that in a dyehouse using both hank- and package-dyeing techniques, principally for acrylic and wool yarns, the cost of the two processing routes is virtually identical. It would thus appear that the advantages in hank processing of:

  — lower capital cost of dyeing machines
  — the elimination of package preparation
are off-set by:

  — the lower payloads from dyeing machines
  — the greater labour required in the dyehouse
  — the slow and labour-intensive hank rewinding operation.

Higher waste factors generally apply to hank processing and, whereas total waste from all processes in package operations may be as low as 1.5%, the waste from hank processing may be as high as 5%. This must have serious financial consequences, especially with high-value yarn.

If modern circular machines are used for dyeing hanks, the cost of dyeing alone will increase dramatically compared to package dyeing in the same machine. Overheads, wages, water, effluent and steam costs will be divided over a smaller weight of hanks. Table 4.7 indicates that, with hanks, loading is only 45% of that for package loading in a given machine.

Thus, in general terms, hank processing is a costly operation in terms of labour and many other factors. Although other alternatives, especially package methods, can be more competitive for cost and product quality, apparently there are cases where hank dyeing gives a yarn whose characteristics cannot be matched as yet by other processing routes.

8.8 CONCLUDING COMMENT

It is hoped that this small contribution will be of value to both the student and established practitioner alike. Yarn dyeing, particularly in package form, is a high-technology process and has a significant part to play in the coloration of textiles. In recent years, major advances have taken place and this pattern will no doubt continue. Research and development work is the life blood of the dyeing and finishing industry and even as this book is completed, it is known that projects are in hand by various organizations to push forward the frontier of the knowledge of yarn dyeing.

Two important objectives for yarn processors must be the elimination of winding operations wherever possible, and definition of those areas in which hank and package processing will yield identical products. In some cases, this may mean changes in yarn engineering, modification of processing routes or alteration of finishing techniques.

The future viability, profitability, efficiency and ultimate survival of the textile industry may well depend on such innovative changes.